Help Me, God! It's Hard To Cope

ROBERT G. TUTTLE

C.S.S. Publishing Company

Lima, Ohio

HELP ME GOD! IT'S HARD TO COPE

4881/ISBN 0-89536-698-3   PRINTED IN U.S.A.

Table of Contents

Dedication

Dedicated to the memory of
three men of great faith:

Robert G. Tuttle Sr. *(my father)*

Dr. Elbert Russell
(former Dean of Duke Divinity School)

Albert Edward Day
(In his time a leader in the spiritual life
of the Methodist Church)

These three men sustained me during times of doubt and struggle which I faced when, as a younger minister I was confronted by the demands of an expanding faith.

Introduction

Too many of us are suffering from burnout. We have allowed life to become too heavy a burden upon us. We are not handling life very effectively, and this depresses us.

There is Spiritual strength available to face any of the demands of life. Too many of us are unaware of this available strength and guidance.

The purpose of this book is to enable us to open the doors of our lives to a healing faith through which we can meet anything that life demands of us. God through Christ is an active force in everyday life. We need to be constantly aware of this.

This book will help the reader face up to those threats of life that tend to break us down, and to find powerful resources for an adequate response.

— Robert G. Tuttle

1

Coping with Fear, Worry, and Anxiety

If you do not worry, if you have never worried, if you do not plan to worry, do not read this chapter; it will be a waste of time. But if a dark cloud of worry overshadows your life, read this chapter carefully; the shadow can be dispelled.

We live in an age of anxiety. The image is the image of fear — not the image of faith. We respond to the old Scotch litany: "From ghoulies and ghosties and long-leggety beasties And things that go bump in the night, Good Lord, deliver us!" It seems that we expect the worst, and we get it.

Leslie Weatherhead, famous English preacher of the closing generation, once shared a helpful insight into the structure of fear. He observed that when an automobile breaks down it is more often the fault of the driver than the fault of the machine. The machine is tough and made to stand a great deal. But the driver of the car gets confused and makes a foolish judgment and the car breaks down — or is wrecked. Occasionally the machine *does* break down, but not so often. Weatherhead declares it is the same with the human body. It is made to stand a great deal of stress. But frequently the "soul-mind," the driver of the body, gets off beam and the body gets sick and breaks down. Doctors and psychiatrists tell us this over and over again. Fear, worry, and anxiety are among the forces that attack the soul-mind and bring about the breakdown of the body.

What about the chemistry of fear? We are told that under the shock of a piano falling on her child it is often possible for a mother to do the impossible and lift the piano off her child. Immediately afterwards she loses that extra strength and cannot budge the piano. What has happened? Under the shock of possible injury to her child, adrenalin has poured into the mother's blood stream, and under the stimulus of this powerful drug she does "the impossible" in order to save the child. This automatic reaction of the glands of our body to extreme and sudden fear can save our lives.

This is not the end of the story. Under the influence of continued anxiety — long-drawn-out fear and dread — the adrenalin continues to seep slowly into the blood stream and poisons us. Eventually it can bring about physical breakdown. That is why a psychiatrist who was concerned about his patients was heard to say, "I wish that my patients could understand that the love, the forgiveness, the care of God is available to them at all times and in all circumstances." This kind of faith counterbalances fear and can bring healing to the physical body.

Doctors agree that emotional stress can bring actual changes in the organs, glands, and tissues of the body. Bio-feed-back is telling us much more in this field. It's not so much "what I'm eating" as "what's eating me" that's getting me down.

But what about subconscious fears? They have been with us a long time. In the book of Psalms a writer cries out, "Why art thou cast down O my soul, why art thou disquieted within me?" Like us, he got up one morning under a heavy cloud of depression and didn't know why. On the other hand, we can get up some mornings elated and buoyed up, and not see any reason for it. Strange forces come up out of the subconscious and attack us. "Our shadows have shadows; our anxieties have anxieties." We stare into the abyss until we topple over and are consumed by it. As one woman wrote to a friend: "I'm seriously considering having a nervous breakdown."

We need not let phobias "scare us to death." Almost everybody has some kind of phobia, and behind many phobias are sensible explanations. When my wife and I started our preaching career, she had a phobia that was worrying her, and I knew nothing about it. She felt like going into a panic when she was crowded. This was a form of claustrophobia. It frightened her. She was afraid she was losing her mind. When crowded in church, she was afraid she would have to run from the building. Her hands would perspire and she was so up-tight that she was exhausted before the service was over.

Finally she told me about it, and of her terrible fear of losing control. I could tell her that in my counseling I had sought to help many persons with similar fears. That helped her to know that there were others, and that she wasn't alone in her fear. When troubled by subconscious fears, it helps to talk them over with someone you trust. We talked about her problem; we prayed about it. She moved from the crowded congregation into the set-apartness of the choir; since she enjoyed singing, the intensity of the phobia began to disappear. She got over it. Now the only thing that disturbs her is getting into a small automatic elevator alone. Regarding these former fears, she is now a free and happy person.

How did her phobia begin? Very possibly like this: as a child she was crowded into a pew at church on a very hot day. Being the smallest in a large family, she felt crushed and overcome by the heat. She knew she could not cry out or run, so she sat and suffered. The trauma sank into her subconscious mind, so that similar crowded situations in the future brought forth the old feeling of terror, even though the original incident had been (so she thought) forgotten.

One psychologist writes of a young woman who was almost beside herself because she was afraid she was losing her mind. This abnormal fear of insanity withdrew her from life and normal relationships. By some fortunate miracle she got married and had six children, one right after the other. To her amazement, at the end of the six overcrowded years, when she had a moment to look at herself, behold! The old fear of losing her mind had totally disappeared. She hadn't had time for it. This prescription is a bit drastic, but such an overwhelming interest or preoccupation is good therapy.

One grandmother tried bringing her three-year-old grandson to church. She was so busy trying to keep him from breaking up the service that she was totally relieved of her own claustrophobia.

There was a young boy in one of the congregations that I served who went into a traumatic fit every night when his parents tried to tuck him into bed. They couldn't understand his behavior. Later they remembered that when the child was a year and a half old he had fallen and received a bad cut, for which several stitches had to be taken. Although the doctor had given him an anesthetic when the stitches were put in, when the time came to *remove* the stitches the doctor had felt that the anesthetic was unnecessary. The child was frightened and would not remain still. The nurse held him to the operating table by the white covering sheet. The child, fearing he was being crushed and smothered, went into a traumatic fit. The stitches were removed. The child "forgot" all about it. But for years the old terrorizing traumatic fears were experienced everytime he was tucked into bed.

Take heart! The subconscious can be positive as well as negative. There is a story of a man in New York City who, when he smelled a certain horrible odor, would go into ecstasy and feel as if he were on cloud nine. He couldn't imagine why, until one day he remembered. As a little boy he would visit his grandfather's farm in the early spring. Barefooted, he would follow his grandfather through the apple orchard as he sprayed the fruit trees. The sky was blue. The little clouds were white. The apple blossoms were pink. The bees were buzzing, and the spray had a terrible stink. But to a little boy the whole experience was heaven, and it sank into his subconscious mind. That memory still caused a wonderful state of euphoria when he caught a whiff of that awful spray in later years.

The subconscious plays strange tricks on us. But by faith in, and assurance from, the caring love at the heart of the universe, our fears can be quieted; and at the heart of our being there can be surprising peace. A patient on vacation illustrated it when writing on a card to her psychiatrist, "Having a good time. Why?"

Worry is an expression of fear and robs us of our full energy for living. Only to a point is the following bit of doggerel an expression of truth:

> Don't worry if you worry,
> Don't let it cause you pain;
> It is vitally normal,
> And absolutely sane.

When worry moves beyond normal concern, it becomes debilitating and even destructive to health. As a young minister I was sent to the "Outer Banks" of North Carolina. I had seven churches up and down the coast. We lived in the house at Kitty Hawk where the Wright brothers had lived when they experimented with their plane and made the first powered flight.

Here, I learned the eclipsing power of worry early in my ministry. I had only one sermon to begin with. I was scared and up-tight. Just as I went into the pulpit for my first service, Mrs. "X" came up to me and said, "Preacher, Mrs. Jones is in the hospital. Now don't forget to see her this afternoon." There I was with a sermon and Mrs. Jones, both on my hands. As I tried to preach, I kept remembering, "Now don't you forget Sister Jones." When I was supposed to be thinking about what I was saying, Mrs. Jones kept interrupting! This left me in a drastic nervous state. Such a mental block coming from trying to hold two things in concentration at once stayed with me for two or three years. It affected my preaching and my peace of mind.

It was solved for me in an interesting way. As I struggled with the conflict, something deep within me said, "God does not expect you to do more than one thing at a time. Now is the moment you have to preach. God can take care of Mrs. Jones until you get through." I tried it. And I have learned that I can always leave the Mrs. Joneses in the hands of God. After the demands of the moment are completed, God has always brought my mind back to Mrs. Jones. I find that I can trust God in little things.

A very fine businessman in a congregation I was serving in later years discovered a simple gimmick to overcome the problem of paralyzing worry. His problem had been that he would start to make an important sale and his mind would jump to a particular unsolved problem. He couldn't shake it off and his sales effectiveness suffered.

He found his release. He began carrying little white cards in his pocket. Whenever a worry would begin to conflict with his concentration on work, he would stop a minute and write the problem down on one of his "worry cards", put it in his pocket, and then go on single-mindedly with his business.

Every Thursday at 2:30 p.m. he would go to his secretary and say: "Don't let anyone disturb me. I am going back to the storeroom to worry." After locking himself in, he would get out his worry cards. This one had already solved itself. This one was not important. These he discarded. There were always a few cards that needed some thought. He worked through these and went out, a free man ready to do one thing at a time.

But worry can go much deeper than this. During the Second World War many of the young men of my congregation were overseas. Some of them lost their lives. I had to carry this tragic news to their families. The whole world scene was a dark shadow. My subconscious mind recorded this darkness, for I developed an ulcer. Now, a minister of Christ should have faith enough not to have an ulcer shouldn't he? I had faith, but it was merely intellectual. I knew in my mind that God was in control and that there was light beyond that darkness. My subconscious mind, which controlled my digestive system, was not convinced, however. The ulcer took over. I tried everything — even milking two milk goats. *

My mind trusted God but my stomach had doubts. It bothered me for several years. But our good God proved stronger than my ulcer. He worked in me when I was not even aware of it. Finally my faith and assurance and peace seeped down into my subconscious, my total inner being, where the fear existed and where the sickness was. There came a deep inner peace that even my stomach could recognize. The burden was lifted. The healing processes that God has built into us began to function and I was healed.

Perhaps that is the meaning of true conversion. The subconscious, the deep total being, suddenly realizes the love, the forgiveness, the peace, the presence of a knowing, caring, competent God. And finally we are free — joyously free!

This is not wishful thinking. All this is based on reality, deep reality. The origin of life is with the Creator-God. The meaning of life is in God. The destiny of life is in his adequate hands. The true values of life were built into us by the Creator, Sustainer God, who is like Christ. At center, the universe is *mind* and *heart*, not machine.

No wonder Jesus kept saying to his disciples, "O ye of little faith." It is said that if Christ would come today into a room of assembled people, and these people would bring to him all their fears, their sins, their sicknesses, their failures, he would say one thing to all of them: "You do not really trust God." Our problem often is, our faith is not fully realized in our total being, where the issues of life and health are rooted. Here it is not so much "what I think" as *what I convincingly feel as certainty* that brings healing.

Often children are closer to reality than we adults are. In a little book of children's "letters to God" there is this:

"Dear God,
       If I was God I wouldn't be as good at it. Keep it up.
                                                                Michelle."

Perhaps the world needs to realize this truth more deeply.

Much of our overwhelming fear comes from our confused thinking about what is real. What is the nature of the universe? What

---

*(The minister who followed me in that congregation was having some difficulty in getting the leaders of the parish to undertake some ministry he felt to be important. In the service one Sunday morning he remarked with some feeling, "No wonder a former minister of yours had to drink goat milk!")

is the character of God? Is not the universe solid? Was it not designed to produce and develop real persons? Can that be accomplished when everything is made easy and is smoothly polished? Something magnificent is being accomplished here and we are a part of it. Somehow Christ comes through to me as Reality, and I trust him.

"Can a Christian be a pessimist?" A student threw this question at me during a college retreat. How would you answer it? I had to think, but then I answered: "No. A person of real faith cannot be a pessimist. He is a realist. Christ was a realist. He saw life as it was. He saw the evil and the good. He was not blind. He saw the sickness and the hate, the lack of love, the injustice, the death and tragedy. And yet, as someone put it, 'he saw God over against the pile of evil, and he was at peace.' Christ was forsaken, spat upon, had a crown of thorns pushed down on his head; he was mocked and crucified, yet he looked at the whole picture and declared 'I have overcome the world.' Christ was a realist, and so is the Christian. Never a pessimist, a realist, sustained by faith."

Once Jesus painted a picture of striking contrast. We have it recorded in Matthew 7:

What then of the man who hears these words of mine and acts upon them? He is like a man who had the sense to build his house on rock. The rains came down, the floods rose, the winds blew, and beat upon that house; but it did not fall, because its foundations were on rock. (NEB)

Then Jesus went on to describe the opposite person, the one who built his house on sand. The same natural elements attacked in the same way and that house fell with great destruction.

What was Jesus trying to say? "He who acts upon these words of mine" — they will endure. Those who have an abiding faith in the God whom Jesus makes clear to us will not be shaken. Whatever life throws at them, they can take. They have an understanding of life and what is back of it. They do not collapse; they are sustained. That is rock!

On the other hand, those persons who have no faith, whose lives are built on nothing that makes sense, collapse because they have no structure of faith, no understanding of life. They go to pieces. Fear is the great destroyer. Faith casts out fear. Subconscious fears eat out the inner strength of life; subconscious faith builds quietly the inner

14

strength and brings peace.

Wherever he went, Jesus was always bringing sanity and health. "Fear not, be not afraid," is Christ's constant word to the disciples and to us. That is ultimate truth speaking. Christ would say to us, "You are able. The Father knows you have need of these things. You can handle any situation that God calls you to. This crisis can be met. God loves you and upholds you. He will not let you down. Ever!"

> *My peace I leave with you, my peace I give unto you. Not as the world giveth give I unto you. Let not your heart be troubled, neither let it be afraid.*

Some amazing insights come to us from the unique faith of a black patriarch. He lived on the Mississippi Delta and his cabin was washed away every few years. Kate McAlpine Grady in the *Southwest Review*, put it into words some fifty years ago. Such faith casts out fear:

> What you gwine-a do when de
> riber overflow?
> Set on my gallery, and watch
> her go.
>
> How you gwine-a ack wid de water
> in your room?
> Sweep it out wid a sedge-straw
> broom.
>
> What you gwine-a do when your
> hawgs all drown?
> Gwine-a wish I lived on higher
> ground.
>
> What you gwine-a do when de
> cow floats away?
> Trow in after her a bale of
> hay.
>
> How you gwine-a ack when de
> cabin leaves?

Climb on de roof and straddle
    de eaves.

What you gwine-a do widout no
    shelta?
Float wid de current down to de
    delta.

How you gwine-a ack when it
    come on night?
Trus in Gawd, and hold on
    tight.

What you gwine-a do if your
    stren'th give way?
Say, "Howdy, Lawd, it's Jedg-
    ment day!"

2

Lifting the Burden of Guilt

"There is a cancerous strain eating away at the average American," writes C. Neil Strait.* He continues, "It is a strain brought on by too much work and too little play; too much hatred and too little love; too much fear and too little faith. The over-balance has infected life with a strain that eats away at the energies of life like a dreadful disease. The strain that besets a lot of people is more a strain of conscience than any other single factor. Because there is a war with conscience, there is a war on all fronts of life."

"God may forgive (our) sins," writes Alfred Korzybski in the *Christian Century*," but (our) nervous systems won't." Unless we find a release, we cannot continue to live with our own particular break with reality. Guilt is a registering of something wrong deep inside me: something doesn't fit, doesn't fit me, doesn't fit life, doesn't fit reality, doesn't fit God.

Recently a Russian author wrote a book, the theme of which was, "If the whole world were covered with asphalt, sooner or later the green grass would break through." If evil and hate are everywhere possessing the world, sooner or later goodness and love will break through. Why? Because these are basic to reality. Guilt is the "scream" of goodness and love denied, both personal and social. We know we have some things for which to answer.

Dr. Edward Stein has written a helpful book, *Guilt: Theory and Therapy*. He says, "Guilt is the peg on which the meaning of man hangs. It is also the peg on which man often hangs himself." Guilt reveals the violation of reality; but an over-played, false, sick

---

*"Strait Lines," *Quote* Magazine, May 2, 1976, p. 425.

subconscious guilt can destroy one's life. Dr. Stein continues: "(Guilt) is the dynamic principle operative in man which verifies the fictitiousness of his total autonomy and the validity of his dependence upon all the rest of life, essentially the human community, and supremely, the source and principle of all life, God . . . " When we break with God and life, guilt is the red warning light that comes on.

"Guilt is the shadow we cast when we walk in the light of God." With these words Fitzsimons Allison reminds us of a child's game that all of us have played: "Escape Your Shadow." When a child first becomes aware of his shadow, he is fascinated by it. He runs; the shadow runs. He jumps; so does the shadow. He falls down; the shadow falls down. He can't escape it. But there *is* one way: run into the darkness and there is no shadow, no contrast. Many persons in today's culture have found that solution. They take shelter in an evil environment where no shadow is cast. But this plunge into total darkness develops into total destruction. There is no saving guilt reaction because we are totally possessed by evil.

Someone has given us a parable. A Jewish family in Nazi Germany knew that soon they would be sent to a concentration camp. They wanted desperately to save their retarded son from this destruction. Therefore, they worked out a bargain with a young German soldier who lived on their street. He was to carry their son into the mountains and protect him. For this service they would deed all their property to him.

The soldier accepted. The couple was taken to the concentration camp. The soldier took the child to the mountains and left him to starve. He took over the family's property and congratulated himself on how clever he was. But the next morning, as he was preparing to shave, he was shocked to discover a bump on his forehead the size of a goose egg. He felt that this bump was declaring his guilt. He pushed and pushed and finally the bump popped in — but it popped out on the back of his head! He pushed and pushed; it popped out on the left side. He pushed again. It popped out on the right side. He pushed again. It popped out on *top* of his head. He put on his hat and went to work. But guilt is not so easily covered up. It is really inside us.

Or we can illustrate it this way. I am driving to a nearby city to attend a meeting. The little red warning light comes on on the dashboard of my car. I'm in a hurry. I can't afford to be late. I kick out the little red light and drive on. But soon my motor is ruined.

18

Not so many of us are so stupid. But we do the same thing with the warning lights that come on in our lives. The guilt experience is a warning light that tells us we are breaking with truth, with reality, with God. Often we cover up our feeling of guilt and continue our destructive practices. How stupid can we get?

Someone in the Fourth Century knew the meaning of guilt and wrote a hymn to it:

O Felix Culpa (O Happy Guilt)

Praise to thee, dear brother Guilt!
Strong Son of God's law and love
Who dost not cease thy pricks
When we would stop to play with dangerous toys
Who goads us from the quicksands of anger and (uncon-
    cern,)
Who makes our hearts to hunger
Beyond new clothes, new chariots, new kitchens,
New houses, new spouses, or even a new Nation.

I have quarreled with thee, O tenacious
    Shadow that I cannot help but cast
    as I walk in God's Light.
I have hated thee as the enemy of my sweet sicknesses.
Thy counterfeits have hurt and wounded me.
    But thou art the Handle of God's Help,
        The Gift of His Grace, and
The image of my health;
Thou, in thy True Self,
Art (my Glory's) True Friend and Brother.
Praise to Thee, O Happy Guilt,
And leave me not 'till we are both at home."

Guilt is real; it has a purpose. How do we face it?

It was three AM. The phone rang and rang until I finally surrendered and lifted the receiver. Out of the darkness came an agonizing cry. Just five short words: "Can I ever be forgiven? Can I ever be forgiven? Can I ever be forgiven?" Only this! How do you answer? I spoke to the one in the darkness: "Yes! Yes, you can be forgiven, if you truly want to be forgiven. All the love of God, all the suffering of

Christ on a Cross say you can be forgiven. Christ says to you now, 'Your sins are forgiven, go and sin no more.' He will forgive you and sustain you." I never found out who called me that night. I hope she got the message and found her peace.

How did Jesus handle those people who came to him paralyzed by guilt? Here is the picture. (Mark 2:1-13) Jesus is preaching to a large crowd in someone's home. Four friends are trying to carry a paralyzed friend to Jesus for healing. The crowd is too great. They can't get near the Master. They climb up on the flat roof and cut a hole through the roof of boughs and dried mud. They let him down right in front of Jesus. It seems that nothing disturbs the composure of the Master. He looks at the paralyzed man, intuitively reads the situation, and says, "Friend, your sins are forgiven."

When some complained that no one could forgive sins but God, Jesus asked, "Is it easier to say, 'Your sins are forgiven' or to say, 'stand up, take up your bed and walk'?" And to convince them of his power to forgive sins, he commanded the paralyzed man, "I say to you, stand up, take up your bed, and go home." And before the astonished crowd, the sick man got up, took up his stretcher, and went out in full view of them all.

Jesus said to the paralytic, whose inner house was so divided against itself that he could not move, "Your sins are forgiven. Your guilt is lifted. Your break with life, your break with truth, your break with God is healed. Get up, get back into life. That's where the Father wants you."

God wants his stumbling children forgiven, healed, and restored to their proper place of responsibility in life. Accept forgiveness, and get on with effective life! Jesus changed the picture all over Palestine. Paralyzed people arose and entered again into full life. "Your sins are forgiven, go and sin no more." This is the source of Guilt redeemed. Guilt redeemed, not pushed under your hat.

Out of his own unbelievable experience of forgiveness, Paul cried out, "Where guilt abounds, Grace much more abounds!" This is the spirit of health and wholeness that God gives, because he loves us.

Jesus told of the son who violated his father's love and went into riotous living, but then decided to return to his father, and was met with open arms. This is the way it is with a forgiving God.

Look at the motion picture, *The Man in the Gray Flannel Suit:* "Like half a million other guys in gray flannel suits, I'll always pretend

to agree, until I get big enough to be honest without getting hurt."
But you don't ever get that big. You go on cheating yourself and
others, until you are smothered by dishonesty. The guilt piles up until
you cannot handle it. "Only he is free who obeys the Divine order
within himself."

Let me share a tragic story. A professional man in a city where I
once served had been following a destructive course in his personal
life. This practice had been hidden but was suddenly revealed to the
entire community. I heard about it and went early in the morning to
visit him. I had rarely seen a person in more agony. During his
all-night struggle, he had literally bitten through his lip. Soon after
this he suffered a paralyzing stroke, and not long after that he was
dead.

God did not want this. At any time in the tragic process, this man
could have told God about it and asked for forgiveness. God would
have forgiven him and restored him. The sad thing was the man had
paid no attention to the warning light of guilt.

"When faith goes out the window," declares Sir John Hilton,
"something else comes up from the drains." We live that close both
to heaven and to hell. In the inner man we touch evil, and we touch
God. Darkness and light, how they fight over our souls! But by the
grace of Christ, your sins *can* be forgiven; you *can* get up and get
back into life. The grass *can* break through the asphalt and live again.

When "I, as-I-am" come to meet "God, as-God-is," my sins are
forgiven; my guilt is healed; I am freed from my paralysis.

Dietrich Bonhoeffer, who was an inspiration to young German
pastors, twenty years ago, just before his execution in a Nazi prison,
confesses his own inner struggle:

Who am I? This or the other?
   Am I one person today and tomorrow another?
Am I both at once?
   A hypocrite before others —
And before myself a woe-be-gone weakling?
   Who am I?
They mock me, these lonely questions of mine.
   Whoever I am
Thou knowest O God,
   I am Thine!

That is the answer. "Whoever I am, Thou knowest O God, I am Thine." When I reach that place of *belonging,* I am forgiven and I am ever being restored. God is working out his ordered life in me. I am in agitated peace.

Many psychiatrists are beginning to recognize that mental break-down comes not from repressing basic instincts, *but from repressing our normal faith in God,* our inner experience of Truth, our inner awareness of a moral order. Cover up the truth, and the truth cries out in many ways. The grass breaks through the asphalt. Faith is the subconscious awareness that God is for us, not against us; that God is not seeking to crush us but to restore us.

I must tell about an old friend of mine. He was ninety-three years old. I sat on his porch one afternoon and he shared his life with me. He said, "It was seventy-two years ago, in 1881. It was a Monday night after the first Sunday in October. I went to a little church where they were having a revival meeting. I was crushed under a burden of guilt, made hopeless under a sense of doom; I could hardly breathe. In despair, I offered myself to Christ, just as I was. The burden was lifted; my sins were forgiven; my life was transformed. That was seventy-two years ago. And to this day I have thanked God for forgiveness and for life, everyday."

Why is this important? I, along with everybody else in that town, knew of the beauty of this man's life, his unselfishness, his love of others. There was no doubt about the reality of that which had happened to him.

In the unforgettable play, *Green Pastures,* during the scene where Christ is stumbling under the burden of the Cross, someone whispers, "It is too terrible a burden for one man to carry." That is true, but all the love of God, all the strength of God was bearing it with him. And so it is with you and me, as we struggle under our particular burden. If we let him, all the love, all the strength of God bears it with us. The suffering of God is tied into the secret of our forgiveness.

I know not how that Calvary's Cross
A world from sin could free,
I only know its matchless love
Has brought God's love to me!

It was, again, three AM. The phone disturbed the peace of the night. A nurse from the hospital was calling to say that there was a man who was not expected to live until morning. He was suffering under a terrible burden of guilt. He was frightened; he was in agony. No one could help him. Would I come?

I went. The sick man could not accept forgiveness. We prayed; he found no peace. The time was short. Something in me said, "He has two sons." That was my cue. I said to him, "If one of your sons had sinned against you grievously, if he would rush into this room at this minute and say, 'I have been false to you; I have let you down. I want to be forgiven. Dad, can you forgive me? Dad, please forgive me. What would you do? Would you turn him down? Or, would you forgive him?"

A look of peace came into his face, a smile crept about his lips. He answered, "I would forgive him."

And I replied, "So also is the forgiveness of the Heavenly Father."

He had gotten the message. He was at peace.

Friend, thy sins be forgiven thee, your break with God is healed. Arise, get back into life.

3

"I Don't Hate Any More!"

A. E. Housman, in a brief verse, uncovers the awfulness of hate:

I see
In many an eye that measures me
The mortal sickness of a mind
Too unhappy to be kind.
Undone with misery, all they can
Is to hate their fellow man;
And till they drop need must still they
Look at you and wish you ill.

That is a plague I would hope to escape.

E. Stanley Jones shares his keen insight into the self-destruction of hate. He reminds us that "a rattlesnake, if cornered, will sometimes become so angry it will bite itself. That is exactly what the harboring of hate and resentment against others is: a biting of oneself. We think that we are harming others in holding these spites and hates, but the deeper harm is to ourselves."

Many times hate and anger are the hidden cause of tragic accidents. On June 18, 1972, a B.E.A. Trident crashed at Heathrow airport, London. As a result, 118 lost their lives. What happened? After the usual intensive investigation it was revealed that the pilot had been unhappy because of the way in which an airline strike had been settled. But there was more: As the pilot took the plane off the ground, he felt the plane to be badly off trim. The men who loaded the cargo had carelessly failed to keep the weight in balance. The pilot, already angry, became furious and over-corrected, jamming his controls. The plane dived into the runway and 118 were killed.

Many one-car accidents are due to anger. A man has had a quarrel with his wife or with his boss. He jumps in his car, and in anger, shoves it to the limit and wrecks it.

It is interesting to note that a good optometrist will not examine the eyes of an angry person. At such a time the retina is distorted by an abnormal blood flow. "I'm so mad I can't see straight" actually makes sense!

Within our bodies vital organs sit in judgment upon our moods and tempers. Hate pumps up our blood pressure. Rage is indigestible. I've tried it and I know. Brain, heart, blood pressure, digestive system form a jury that quickly condemns our blighting bitterness and our consuming resentments. Even tissue changes take place. For these reasons some doctors say that it is not pills their patients need, *but the grace that will enable them to forgive.*

Smouldering hatred can destroy you; forgiveness can bring healing. I attended a men's breakfast in a community into which I had just moved. Sitting next to a man I had never seen, I discovered that he was a member of our congregation. I also learned that he was on the verge of a severe heart attack and that his doctor had released him from the hospital to attend the breakfast. As we talked, I sensed his uptightness and suggested that he come by my office to talk after breakfast. He accepted. In the conversation, I realized that he was burning mad at his boss.

I said, "You hate your boss, don't you?"

"Yes, I do," he answered, "but I wasn't really aware of it."

It developed that he was a used-car salesman. He was honest by nature. His boss was forcing him to misrepresent the cars he was selling. He hated it; he hated himself; he hated his boss.

At the close of the interview, I suggested that we pray: that we pray for his boss, and then that *he* pray for his boss. This was tough, but he did it. By the close of the prayer he had relaxed. His facial expressions were different. He went back to the hospital, and they dismissed him. He told his boss that he had hated him for his business practices. He quit his job and got another. He was reconciled to his family and began to live a creative life in the community. His experience was much like that of a young doctor in a fellowship group who suddenly stood up and declared joyously, "I don't hate any more! I don't hate any more!"

He didn't have to like what his boss was doing; he could hate the boss's crooked practices, but he could also care for his boss as a person and want him to become an honest man with whom others could work and whom they could admire. This new attitude toward his boss, discovered as he prayed for him, set my friend free and his health began to return.

This is why Jesus admonished his followers, "Bless them that curse you, pray for them that despitefully use you and persecute you." It sounds "way out," but it works.

On another occasion Jesus said: "If you are on the way to worship at the Temple, and you remember that your brother has something against you, leave your gift. Go be reconciled with your brother, and then come and offer your gift." (Matthew 5:23-24)

You cannot worship with a lump in your soul. You cannot receive an inflow of love except as you share in an outflow of love. Our unforgiveness blocks the flow of God's love. The Lord's Prayer is serious business: "Forgive us our sins as we forgive others." In other words, it could mean, "I am not going to forgive, Lord; therefore, do not forgive me."

One more illustration comes from a friend of mine. His friend was very ill in the hospital. The doctors gave little hope. I had an outstanding layman coming as guest speaker in our city. My friend asked if I would allow him to take this Christian layman to visit his sick friend. They went to the hospital together. The layman talked with the sick man. By chance (or providence) he mentioned a situation in his own life.

"A year ago," he said, "I was sick. My brother had cheated me. I hated him. It was destroying me. By some miracle, I was enabled to forgive my brother. The awful load of hate was lifted, and I was free. My health returned."

The sick man rose up in the bed and almost shouted: "How did you know I hated my brother? I hate him, I hate him, and it's killing me. I know it's not natural to hate your brother."

They prayed for the hated brother, that God might change him into a creative, good person, and take the evil from him. The sick man was released. He began to improve, and soon his health was restored. In this context, Jesus' words make surprisingly good sense: "Love your enemies, do good to them that hate you, and despitefully use you."

Sometimes little boys think in distressingly adult ways. A minister once asked a small boy: "Son, what would you do if another boy would slap you on the right cheek"? The little fellow looked up with a questioning expression and asked, "How big is he?" Often we put conditions on the commands of God.

"To forgive is always there and always necessary — especially when it seems so unfair to have to," Max Sullins reminds us. "Forgive seventy times seven": live in a constant spirit of forgiveness. It is the healing spirit.

One fact might be helpful to remember: The hurter is in greater need than the one who is hurt. If you are being gossiped about or slandered, the evil is external. But the one who is harming another is an agent of evil and is possessed by evil. The hurter is in greater need of help than the hurt. Pray for them that despitefully use you.

What are the "mechanics of anger"? An automatic tightening of the fists, a constriction of the throat, a shortness of breath (you are breathing faster), a raising of the pitch of your voice, a rigidity of the muscles — all these are inbuilt, automatic preparations for a fight or for flight. These are protective devices.

But what of anger that turns to hatred? It becomes a long-drawn-out burning. The adrenalin is played out slowly into the blood stream; the nervous system remains tense and up-tight; bodily functions are thwarted; and health is broken. "It just burns me up" really expresses it.

Revenge is not "sweet." I've tried it. "Boy, did I get even with him! I really got him!" Afterwards I see how little I am, and I don't like myself.

God gives us a way out: "Vengeance is *mine*. I will repay, sayeth the Lord." Vengeance is not our business. God is just; God knows the score; God will do what is right. On this basis I might be sorry for the one who hurt me; he has hurt himself, or herself, even more.

Remember, it is not easy to be kind and forgiving in this kind of world. Our grandfathers had lots of room. They could do pretty well as they pleased on their property. But today we live house to house: we work elbow to elbow; we drive fender to fender. That's tough. We get in each other's way.

This bit of doggerel by R. Em Marino throws light on today's tensions:

The courts will judge this sorry case:
How two men squared off, face to face,
How words could not control their pace,

How both men rolled in harsh embrace,
How two good citizens fells from grace,
And neither got the parking space.

Hatred can fill our thoughts with contradictions. A wife wrote to her husband:

> "Dear George,
> ˉI hate you.
>   Love, Alice"

We need more of the saving grace of forgiveness than our grandfathers ever did.

Clergy are not exempt. As a young preacher in my first congregation. I collided head-on with hatred. There was an old. ugly. twenty-foot hedge between the parsonage and the next house. During the Great Depression as it was, a poor man came by wanting work. I had an inspiration. I gave him a saw and told hiim to cut that hedge down to two feet. I went on about my business. When I came home at lunch my young wife was crying. My neighbor had come over and cussed her out. Was I mad! Thereby developed an "international situation" that took some of the grace of God to settle.

The facts were these: The hedge was two inches on my neighbor's side of the line. He had planted it there on purpose. He didn't like preachers! He had placed the hedge there so he wouldn't seem too close. And now I had cut it down! By the grace of mutual forgiveness we worked it out.

These lines by Emily Dickinson offer exciting possibilities for healing:

> Will you tell me my fault
> As frankly as to yourself?
> For I had rather wince than die.
> Men do not call the surgeon
> To commend the bone
> But to set it, Sir.
> And fracture within is more critical.

A spirit of frank honesty and a constant. forgiving spirit make a great combination for healthy, joyful living.

28

Now we look within the depths of our own lives:

Do you have a hate problem?
Are you carrying a grudge?
Are you harboring some deep resentment?
Is bitterness tying up your digestive system?
Is smouldering anger pumping up your blood pressure?

Face it!
Go be reconciled!

Perhaps we need to analyze the situation:

How did it start?
Does the other person know about it?
Do they know how you feel?
Did they do it intentionally?
What is their background?
(Perhaps they haven't had the opportunities we had)
Was there any provocation on your part?
Have you admitted your share of the guilt?
If the situation had been reversed,
    would you have done the same thing?
Have you tried to effect reconciliation?
Have you written to them?
Do you speak to them?
Do you keep the door open to reconciliation?
Do you act toward them with good will?
Do you pray for them?

Don't be like the man who, when an old friend met him on the street saying, "Here, Jim, is that $10 I've been owing you," replied, "Keep it. I'd rather keep on hating you!"

Facing up to our break with someone could bring reconciliation. A meaningful friendship could be restored. When you check it out you might discover that the whole thing was trivial and ought to be forgotten. Or the disagreement might turn out to be significant, and need to be worked out. Say your prayers and to go the person and work it through. Approach them prayerfully, taking a little more than your part of the blame. There could be a great healing.

On the other hand, the other person could slam the door in your face, reject your approach, and have nothing to do with you. All you can do then is "Leave them to God." Let God deal with them. You tried. You acted toward them with good will. You've done all you can. You're free! "I don't hate any more!" God might make something of it yet.

Our three small children had had a real brother-sister fight. They had gone to bed mad at each other. In the middle of the night a terrifying thunderstorm hit our town. The children were awakened. During the worst of the storm I went upstairs to see how they were getting on. I went to Betty's room. No Betty! To Robert's room. No Robert! To Kitty's room. No Kitty! What was wrong? Then I heard, above the storm, some muffled sounds in one of the big hall closets. I opened the door, and there were the three children, huddled in a dark corner. I asked, "What in the world are you doing in this closet." The answer came, "We're in here forgiving each other."

The storm had been fierce. They knew it wasn't best to meet God hating each other. Thunderstorms sometimes clear the air in more ways than one.

In spite of Blondie's convoluted logic, she was on the right track when she said, "Dagwood, if you'll say I'm right, I'll say I'm wrong."

But there is another possibility. What if the case refuses to be resolved? The trouble persists. Insult is added to injury. The thorn in the flesh is deliberately twisted, day by day. What can you do?

A young Christian mother came to me for counseling. She had moved in next door to a woman with an inferiority complex. The neighbor was mad because she, having had little education, felt inferior. In personal warfare she was a genius. Her imagination had no limits. Day after day she planned new insults to irritate her neighbor.

The young mother who came to me for counseling planted a nice hedge along the mutual border. The bitter neighbor dug it up, immediately. Then my counselee planted flowers along the border. The spiteful neighbor uprooted them. The neighbor heard that the young mother was having some company, friends she prized highly. She came up with a new approach. She gathered all the old clothes, ragged clothes, old rags, dirty rags, and hung them on the fence between the two properties. The young mother was sick. It hurts to be reminded day by day that someone hates you and takes joy in hurting you.

What can a Counselor do? I told her to pray for her neighbor, to wish her well, to show her kindness. She did, but it did not help. The mother came back to me in despair. She was sick and developing an ulcer. What could she do?

We prayed. I said, "We've done all we can. But there is one other thing. Before Jesus left his disciples, he said to them, 'My peace I leave with you: my peace I give unto you. Not as the world giveth, give I unto you. Let not your heart be troubled, neither let it be afraid.' This is a divine offer of peace in spite of circumstances. It is a sheer gift. Not like men give, it is a gift from God. Can you bring yourself to receive this gift in the midst of your tension? Can you open yourself to it?"

She opened herself. She received. The whole situation began to be different. The tension relaxed. The old irritation didn't bother her any more. She found she could forget it. The spiteful neighbor began to feel the lack of tension. She began to ease up. She began to open up. Friendship developed across that no-man's land. They began to do things for each other. The spiteful neighbor began to go to church with the neighbor who had now become a friend. Now they live in mutual helpfulness. A miracle! It was a gift of God's Peace.

Christians need to build the bridges that can restore broken human relations. They are the ones who have the resources. Christians should be the ones to take the first steps.

By the grace of God we begin to love (not necessarily "like") difficult people. The bitterness is gone. I don't hate any more. Now I can bring my gift and get through to God, because I have let him get through to me. We have peace (His Peace) in spite of difficult circumstances. The lump has left my soul. I am free. There is no barrier between me and other persons; therefore there is no barrier between me and God.

By grace, you and I have become a part of God's healing, redeeming force at work in the life of our world.

"Pray for them that despitefully use you!"

"Forgive seventy times seven!"

4

Overcoming Loneliness

In the overcrowded conditions of our modern world loneliness has possessed us:

"He's a real Nowhere Man,
Sitting in his Nowhere Land,
Making all his Nowhere Plans
    for nobody."

Such emptiness, such frustration, such loneliness depresses us. What's to be done about it?

This feeling of hopelessness has been around a long time. The ancient writer of the 22nd Psalm cried out:

Dear God, right now I feel like a worm, not a person.
I feel so used by other people. And to make it worse,
I feel resented by the very same people who use me!
Sometimes when my back is turned,
    I can feel everyone making faces at me,
    sneering in derision.
O God, stick close to me — I'm up to my neck in problems
    and all alone.
I feel like the walls are closing in around me.
    And in the dark I can see starving lions ready to
    swallow me up and digest me into oblivion.
My strength drains away like water,
    And my bones feel loose and shaken.
My heart feels like a lump of hot sticky wax

32

melting inside my chest.
My mouth is as dry as a broken piece of clay pot,
    And my tongue sticks to my jaw.
I feel trampled and beaten.

This Psalm is paraphrased by Kenneth W. Chalker in a little book, *Dare to Defy*. He goes on to suggest that even though it may have been written by King David, today it could fit a frustrated homemaker, a retired person, an unemployed person, a beleaguered executive, a worried union leader, a minister or a doctor. All of us, at times, feel that the world has left us, and we are left alone to fight it out. Remember, fathers can be lonely; mothers can be lonely; children and youth can be lonely.

Alan Patan, in his autobiography, *Towards the Mountain*, describes something he saw when he visited Alcatraz:

"Six of these (cells) were shining bronze cages and had no secrets from guard or visitor. But six were sealed behind massive bronze doors, each with its judas hole. I looked through one and could see a man sitting motionless on a bed, beyond all human power to move or touch or make laugh or weep. He was there because he would kill if any chance were given him, because he was possessed, day in and day out, during every hour of working and sleeping too perhaps, by a hatred that consumed him without ceasing . . . was his soul unconquerable?" Was it?

Marlene Patterson in "Alive Now" writes:

Today, I have had another lonely day, Lord.
The one phone call I received was a wrong number.
Was there someone that needed a call from me? . . .
My neighbors wave as they go about their tasks
But we seldom take time to talk . . .
At church we sit in the same pews with people we do not
    know.
Are they lonely too? . . .
Our marriage has been good but sometimes I expect my
    husband to sense my aloneness . . .
Am I lonely because I am afraid to risk reaching out to
    another?"

This old world cries out in many languages. Reuel Howe, in his book *Creative Years*, reveals the inner struggle of a family:

> "It's hard to think straight about our family, we seem so messed up. Wonder if others are like us?
>
> "Julie and I tried to help Bernard and Jane. There's sure a big gap between wanting to do something and doing it. Something gets into kids in their adolescence that makes them harder to understand and to handle. Bernard was defiant, as if he were trying to prove something. It was as if he had a chip on his shoulder and dared me to knock it off. I couldn't figure out whether he was making a bid for more discipline or whether I wasn't giving him enough freedom . . . I failed him as a father without knowing why. He had a way of making me awfully mad. It's funny how the feeling of helplessness makes you angry. Then I'd feel guilty about it all. We lost touch with each other during his teens. Something came between us. I've often wished we could get it out in the open and talk about it. Now lately things seem a little better . . ."

Love is the absolute essential as we confront the world in its loneliness. Bruce Larson, in *There's a Lot More to Health Than Not Being Sick*, draws information from Dr. James Lynch:

> Dr. Lynch's studies show that twice as many white divorced males under age seventy who live alone die from heart disease, lung cancer, and stomach cancer. Three times as many men in this category die of hypertension and seven times as many of cirrhosis of the liver. He also points out that among divorced people, suicide is five times higher and fatal car accidents four times higher."

"Love or perish," says psychologist Smiley Blanton. And Karl Menninger adds, "Love is the medicine for the sickness of the world." Bruce Larson continues with some statistics from a foundling home in Brazil: "The infants there received excellent care. The conditions were sanitary. There was an adequate staff to provide all physical and dietary needs. But there was not enough staff to provide physical love, to simply hold the babies, touch them, play with them. Most of the babies died before the end of the first year."

34

My father, a United Methodist minister, said to me, "I cannot
bear to face another move alone." Mother had died ten years before.
He was moved; he was dead within a year.

An English preacher, writing in *The Expository Times*, tells of
coming out of an eye clinic and seeing "a very modern looking
young woman, her eye all shrouded in a bandage. She stopped
when she came to a pram where the baby was crying lustily, gave the
pram a wee 'shuggle' and said softly to the baby: 'Ssh! Mummy's
coming!' At once the baby stopped crying and soon the girl passed
on. Her little word of comfort — probably the only word the baby
knew — 'Mummy' — had brought reassurance, so the crying
stopped." In a world of lonely people, we often forget to speak that
healing word.

We rush on, not daring to disturb the "sounds of silence":

> And in the naked light I saw
> Ten thousand people, maybe more.
> People talking without speaking,
> People hearing without listening,
> People writing songs that voices never shared,
> No one dared
> Disturb the sounds of silence.

> — Paul Simon,
> *Sounds of Silence*

No wonder we are lonely.

After quoting Paul Simon, Dr. James J. Lynch, in *The Broken
Heart*, goes on to declare, "Quite literally, we must either learn to
live together or face the possibility of prematurely dying alone . . .
Cancer, tuberculosis, suicide, accidents, mental disease — all are
significantly influenced by human companionship. Nature uses many
weapons to shorten the lives of lonely people. On a statistical basis it
simply chooses heart disease most frequently."

Dr. Lynch compares the death rate in Nevada, "number one in
the way it shortens white people's lives in the U.S.," with
neighboring Utah, "which has one of the lowest death rates in the
country. The two states are much the same in wealth and education
and other features. The difference? Utah is extremely religious.
Mormons do not drink or smoke. They generally maintain stable
lives. Marriages are generally secure, family life strong, and most of

the state's people stay in Utah. Nevada is the opposite. It is one of the divorce capitals of the U.S. More than 20 percent of Nevada's males age 35-64 are single, widowed, divorced or not living with spouses. Most Nevadans are born somewhere else — most of those over 20 who live in Utah were born in the State."

Dr. Lynch gloomily declares that Nevada seems to be a prophecy of things to come for the U.S. "Divorce, mobility, living alone, unprotectedness, these have now become acceptable middle-class norms throughout the U.S.," he says.

Dr. Desmond Morris' book, *Intimate Behaviour*, gives us a tip on healing intimacies in human relationships. "We laugh at educated adults who pay large sums to go and play childish games of touch and hug in scientific institutes . . . How much easier it would be if we could accept the fact that tender loving is not a weakly thing, only for infants and young lovers, if we could release our feelings, and indulge ourselves in an occasional and magical return to intimacy." This had its start a long time ago: "And the Lord said, It is not good that man should be alone. I will make a helpmate for him." (Genesis 2:18)

There is an old Swedish proverb: "Shared joy is a double joy. Shared sorrow is half a sorrow."

The wisdom of Paul Tournier in his book, *Reflections*, supports this thesis. "Modern man, despite appearances, is less aware of his own nature and motives, and is lonelier as he faces them. We pity the savage amid his mysterious, menacing spirits, but at least he shares his fears with all his tribe, and does not have to bear the awful spiritual solitude which is so striking among civilized people."

And now Touriner points the lonely ones to faith, "Why does the Bible so often speak of the 'living' God? Surely it is because the God it reveals to us is not the God of the philosophers, outside time and space . . . He is a living person, a person whose voice breaks in upon us, who himself intervenes, who acts, who suffers, who enters history in Jesus Christ, who enters into men by the Holy Spirit." It is only as I have grown older that God has become an intimate Person to me. It makes all the difference.

"People often say to me," continues Tournier, " 'I don't seem to be able to say my prayers; what ought I to do?' I reply: 'Talk to God as you are talking to me; even more simply, in fact.' St. Paul writes that the truest prayer is sometimes a sigh. A sigh can say more than could be contained in many words." With a yearning, a hunger, a cry, the lonely soul reaches out to God and finds comfort.

Why do we insist on doing it by ourselves and stumble inadequately? Things go wrong. We struggle to put things right. We fail again. At last we come back to God and say, "Take over; I can't manage it on my own." Strangely, life begins to work.

When we are lonely, we might remember what Tournier said in, *Escape From Loneliness*, "Love always means going to others, not demanding that they come to us." He continues in, *The Adventure of Living*, "It was for love that God created the world. It was for love that God made man in his own image, thus making him a partner in love, a being to whom he speaks, whom he loves like a son, and who can answer him and love him like a father. It is for love that God respects man's liberty, thus taking upon himself the formidable risk of man's mistakes and disobediences, the price of which he himself accepts and pays in the sacrifice of the cross."

In this busy, stressful world we put ourselves in little boxes and close them on all sides. We must remember, if we are to break out of the prisons of our loneliness, that "the highest sign of friendship is that of giving another the privilege of sharing our inner thoughts." This is the healing power of the small sharing group.

Dr. Tournier comforts us with his own confession: "There is in me the doctor who believes passionately in his medicine, and eagerly runs to help his fellowmen; there is in me the egoist and skeptic who would like to run away and hide in a solitary cabin." But, thank God, he didn't! He goes on to warn us against too much self analysis: "As you peel an onion, there is always another layer, but you never reach the kernel. So, when you analyze the ego, it disappears completely." Many lonely people have gazed inwardly upon themselves until there is nothing there that is visible — and they are canceled out.

The Transforming Friendship, a small book written by the great London minister, Lesle D. Weatherhead, is a very practical approach to the cure of loneliness. Weatherhead, tells us that Christ operates today not so much from the Sea of Galilee as from the Thames, the Potomac, the Hudson. Christ is where people are, where the need is. Weatherhead speaks of Christ visiting a successful business executive. The businessman wanted to show Christ the church where he worshipped. "No," said Christ, "I want to see the place where you work. What are the conditions there? How do the people who work for you get along?" After the visit of Christ that business became more people-conscious.

Then Weatherhead follows Jesus as he visits a home. He shows a special interest in the children and takes time with them. The mother unburdens her heart to Jesus. He listens, never interrupting. The mother laid her problems before him. It was a long list: the dreary hours of housework, meals, cleaning, social obligations, money problems, what might become of the children, how to find time really to teach them the ways of life.

Jesus asked questions about ideals in the home, what they believed in, what they stood for, what were their ideals for the children? And very quietly he spoke to the mother about an inward peace. Jesus reminded her that her entire family was in God's hands; in quietness, and through trusting him, God will give the strength she needs. After his visit there was a glow and a warm sense of peace in all the relationships of that family.

Now Weatherhead leads us into the small room of a university student. The young man was seated alone. He seemed to be a fine athlete. The student was lonely and his heart was heavy. His mind was divided, one side at war with the other. Good and Evil were in a constant tug-of-war for the possession of his soul.

Suddenly Jesus was sitting there in the room. Quietly he spoke, saying, "You thought of me, and so I am here." The student could see that Jesus really believed that he had great potential, and that he would back him up. Thinking deeply, the student whispered, "I will begin again; it's all right now." The next day the vulgar pictures had been taken down from the walls, the fresh air was flowing through the room, and the sunlight had reached the dark corners.

The next picture that Dr. Weatherhead brings into focus is that of "a girl living in a small boarding-house in the city. It was not a pleasant life . . . It was very lonely." The picture reveals the sordid details of her drab life: early in the morning she goes to work in a workroom over a large shop downtown. Every night she is alone. She is getting older and knows very few people. Since there is nothing to do at night, often she will put on her gayest things and go out all alone. She has almost no money, and in her frustration she faces temptation again and again.

She is there in her bare little room. She is leaning over a small table, her face buried in her hands; she is shaking with sobs. Suddenly she looks up, and Jesus is standing there beside her. She is confused, but Jesus puts her at ease by asking, "Would you like to tell me all about it?" She begins to pour out all her troubles, but, looking at Jesus, she senses that he knows about them already. Even though she knows he is aware of her temptations and her selfishness, his presence does not frighten her; hope begins to dawn. She even dares to ask the Master, "What do you see in me?" He answers, "I see the possibilities of beautiful womanhood. I see the potential of a life committed to God." "But don't you see," she insists, "the ugliness, the greed, and things even worse than that?" Jesus answers, "I see far below the surface a real desire for goodness, and a hatred of all that is ugly in life." But she continues, "I have broken my good resolutions; I have lost my chance; my ideals are gone; my faith is no longer meaningful." Jesus looks at her tenderly and whispers, "The Son of Man came to seek and to save that which was lost."

Suddenly she was young again; springtime had returned to her soul. As the vision faded, she heard him say, "You will never be alone again; every day I am with you."

All of us need the kind of comfort Dr. Weatherhead tells us about; we need to be aware of the reality of the Presence of Christ that he suggests. The aloneness we experience is a conscious and subconscious awareness of a separation from God. We can be alone when we are crowded, alone when we stand next to each other. We can be inwardly marooned. Bishop Hazen Werner tells of a woman who said to him, "I live on an island, my husband lives on an island, and neither of us can swim." Perhaps we live in a maze of "organized loneliness." There are strangers outside and the stranger within.

From the bottomless pit of our aloneness, we cry out to one another, but we cannot get the message through. In all the trauma of *Captains and Kings*, Taylor Caldwell has one of her characters remark, "His real need, his most terrible need, is for someone to listen to him." Man will not die from lack of vitamins or lack of shelter; it's loneliness that's killing us. Deep within all of us there is a message crying out to be spoken. But as Jesus said, "people have no eyes to see, no ears to hear." If we would only listen to each other, much of the world's violence would disappear in new levels of personal and corporate understanding.

But we separate ourselves; we build a wall around us, as if we really like our cell. Listen to one such pitiful person:

"Anybody can make himself lonely:

He can allow himself to grow so sensitive that he lives in
    constant pain;
He can nurse his grudges until they are an intolerable
    burden;
He can think himself insulted until he is apt to be;
He can believe the world is against him until it is;
He can imagine troubles until they become real;
He can hold so many under suspicion that he trusts no one;
He can question the motives of his friends until he has no
    friend.

(source unverified)

No one can love a *mask*. If you can't see each other, you can't know each other; if you can't know each other, you can't love each other.

Love, by its nature, cannot respond to command. It responds to love. Perhaps this is our breaking point with God and with life. Sin is not just one or two bad things we do or do not do. As Jesus saw it, it is far more than this: Sin is the rejection of God's Spirit; it is the refusal of love; it is the blocking of joy in human relationships; it is the failing to move toward wholeness of life. Sin is rejecting God's offer of companionship. This leaves a terrible emptiness.

Isolation can be set up by a conflict of freedoms. There is the question: "What am I doing with my freedom? What is my neighbor doing with his freedom? Is my neighbor's freedom a threat to my freedom and my freedom a threat to his? Or might it be possible that his freedom is a support to my freedom and my freedom is a support to his freedom? To understand and to be understood is the open door out of isolation.

Some people take a devilish joy in not liking people. In his book, *How to Live 365 Days a Year*, Dr. John A. Schindler says, "Some people dislike everybody: They dislike practically everyone from the President, whom they have never met, to their next-door neighbor whom they wish they had never met." But can we afford to see everyone as a walking irritant? Can we afford to be so sorry for ourselves that we leave no room for anyone else to be sorry for us?

We rub shoulders with lonely folk every day. In some we recognize it; in some we would never guess it. I remember one of the most exuberant persons I have ever known. He was on the staff of a well-known prep school where I was teaching and coaching track. I was amazed to discover that his wife had left him, and almost

40

everything in his life was tragic. The list goes on: There are the sick ones, the disabled, those who have lost loved ones, those who have nervous problems, complexes, phobias, those who are out of their environment, who have moved to the city and have not found their place there. They are the ones who have not learned to bridge the gap existing between themselves and other persons. They find themselves alone in a sea of persons.

Any of us can wake up in the dead of night with a sense of separation, uneasiness, detachment. It could be a warning — a warning that we are on the wrong track, that we are losing contact with reality, that we have broken with God and with people. It could be the shock that brings us back to a *shared life*. The walls we have erected between us and God separate us from others; the walls we have erected between us and others separate us from God.

Dwelling constantly upon the loss which is behind us can become a sickness. Turning the light ahead, focusing upon the future, getting back into the stream of life can break the spell of aloneness. Take a hint from the lightning bug:

> The Lightning Bug is brilliant,
> But he hasn't any mind;
> He flies about the universe
> With his headlight on behind.

At this point, Dr. Schindler speaks again: "Lose a friend, seek a new one. Keep cheerful. Don't gripe except when no one can hear you. Don't keep talking about how tired you are. If you lack love and affection from others, give more than your share to others. If you lack creative expression, pursue a new interest as though your life depended upon it. If you lack recognition, give recognition to others. Some of it will come back. If you lack experiences, be planning something all the time. (The exhausted housewife meant it when she said, "I'd scream if I didn't have that trip coming up next month!") Get out into the midst of people and discover that they need you as much as you need them."

The only ones who will be really happy are those who have sought and found how to serve. Once I visited an old woman, a practical nurse, in the hospital. Life had been rough on her, and yet she wasn't about to give up. She told me about the hundreds of babies she had helped to deliver. She said, "I never went into a sick room I didn't see something I could do." She had joined the human race; she was on the team; she was in a cosmic partnership; she was a part of history; she was involved in her work; God was involved in her work; she had become a part of the healing of the world. Loneliness can be a rejection of life, or it can become the challenge to free others from loneliness. In loneliness some have discovered humanity.

> The big banana said
> To the little banana,
> 'Stick to de bunch Bud,
> Stick to de bunch,
> Or you're gonna get peeled.'

"To know God and men as friends," said Nels Ferre, "is the very aim and nature of right religion." The old sea Captain had the right spirit:

> If I ever reach my home again
> Where the earth has sky and the sky has rain,
> I'll dig a well for the passers-by,
> Where none shall suffer from thirst as I.

> (Whittier)

Corrie ten Boom had a right to sulk in aloneness, but she didn't; she served others wherever she was. She risked her life and found life abundant. Christ said to her and to us, "I stand at your door and knock." "I will not leave you comfortless. I will come to you." We are lifted by the loneliness of God.

Once I prayed because I ought to. Then I prayed because I needed to. Now I pray because I want to. "Though the outward man perish, the inward man is renewed, day by day."

Gerhard Terstugen puts it,

> Within, within oh turn
> Thy spirit's eye to learn . . .
> Thy dearest friend dwells deep
>   within thy soul,
> And asks thyself of thee.

That he may give himself *to* thee!

In the play, *Green Pastures*, De Lawd said to Gabriel:

"Don't forget about dat star."
"Yes, Sir, I'll take care of it."
"And Gabriel, remember bout dat little sparrow
    with the broken wing."
"Not even a bird falls except your heavenly Father knows
    about it."

Are you alone? Remember the Bible verses you learned as a child:

"Whither shall I flee from thy presence?
"If I ascend up into Heaven, thou art there;
If I make my bed in Hell, behold thou art there.
"If I take the wings of the morning, and dwell in the
    uttermost parts of the sea; even there shall thy right hand
        hold me.
"If the darkness covers me, even the night shall be as light
    about me."

(Psalm 139)

"He that keepeth thee will neither slumber nor sleep . . .
"The Lord shall preserve thee from all evil:
    He shall preserve thy soul.
"He will preserve thy going out,
And thy coming in, from this time forth, and even forever
    more."

(Psalm 121)

Christ says, "I am with you always." Yes, I have felt it!

Our Father in Heaven is both personal and near. When we truly experience this (and he wants us to), we will never be alone again.

5

A Good God and the Problem of Suffering

"I don't know what to do about them, they won't get out of the way."

"Who?" said Stef.

"There's disaster rolling down the hill and they won't move."

"Who won't? Whom are you talking about?"

"I can't make them pay attention, they just stand there . . ." Steinbeck sounded as if he might break into tears. "They won't heed me . . ."

Stef was growing irritable. "Who?" he repeated. "What are you lamenting? Who won't move?"

"My characters!" Steinbeck exploded. He was writing *Of Mice and Men.*[1]

This could be God speaking about us, his children. "We just won't move." We won't listen. We won't think, and accidents, breakdowns, nuclear wars and the like rush down upon us like an avalanche.

But, certainly, this does not totally answer the question of suffering. No! It is only a part of the answer.

On his death bed my father asked me to read him the Book of Job. It brought him comfort. This ancient story throws much light on the problem.

You remember it. There was an Eastern prince, very wealthy, a good man. There was no warning. As Job sat under the shade of his tent one bright morning, looking out across his herds and his grazing

[1] Ella Winters in *And Not to Yield*, Harcourt, Brace and World, 1963.

lands, his attention was caught by a tiny swirl of dust moving across the plain. Soon the dust was seen to be a messanger running. The exhausted runner fell at Job's feet and cried out, "Your oxen were plowing and your asses beside them. The Sabeans have fallen upon them and carried them away, and have slain your servants with the sword. I, only I, am left to tell you."

Even as the first messenger lost consciousness, there came another swirl of dust, another messenger, with another message: "Fire has fallen from heaven and has consumed your sheep and your shepherds with them, and I, only I . . ."

At that same moment came still another messenger: "The Chaldeans, the Chaldeans, have fallen upon your camels and carried them away, and have slain your camel drivers, and I alone am left."

Another cloud of dust, another messenger, another message of woe: "Thy sons and thy daughters . . ." — Job held his breath — "They were all feasting in your eldest son's house and a great wind from the desert has destroyed the house and all your sons and daughters with it."

For a moment the shock was too great for Job. But as he came to himself he whispered, "The Lord has given, the Lord has taken away, blessed be the name of the Lord." Job kept his Faith.

Now what is back of this story? According to the Book of Job, God and Satan met. God asked, "Have you seen my servant, Job? He's a good man."

With a sneer Satan answered, "Oh, yeah! He's rich. He's got everything. Who wouldn't be good with his advantages?"

God replied, "I still believe in him. Take his riches, but *do not touch him.*" You see, God allows Evil certain powers but *keeps control* himself. Evil has power to hurt but God holds evil *under limits.*

After Job had stood the first test, placed on him by the forces of evil, God and Satan had further conversation: God said, "You see, you took all he possessed, and Job is still a person of faith."

"Yeah!" Satan replied. "He's still got his health. You let me touch his body and then you'll see whether he's good or not."

"I still have complete confidence in Job," God answered. "You may make him sick, but you *cannot take his life.*"

Satan struck quickly, afflicting both Job's body and spirit. He was covered with boils. Perhaps he was afflicted with shingles. His wife said, "Give up, curse God and die!" Job was forced to live on the garbage heap. His affliction was complete; he had struck bottom.

Job's misery has been experienced in every generation. The forces of evil continue to attack persons in thousands of ways. But God continues to support his children limiting the forces of evil.

I like Robert Browning, but he misses the point in "Pippa Passes":

> "God's in his heaven,
> And *all's right*
> With his world."

No! All is *not* right within the world. I know better. Anybody knows better. Death, suffering, cancer, tragedy, fighting, violence, nuclear threat, earthquakes, tornadoes, nature gone wild, neglected children, broken homes, torture, alcohol, drugs, and a thousand other things. Does it make sense? On the surface, not much!

Almost anything can happen to almost anybody almost anytime! Even to good people it can happen — to me, to you! God does not bribe us to be good; he undergirds us in the struggle of life. Into this kind of world Christ came. He identified with our suffering. He invaded life with love.

But why do bad things happen to good people? There are some things you can put your finger on: Evil in the world, carelessness, ignorance, selfishness, injustice, sin, hate, germs, natural disaster, wars, mystery. But why? Job wanted to know; I want to know; everybody wants to know.

Why? A fine couple in our town were taking a pleasant drive in the evening; two drunks, coming around a curve at seventy miles per hour, hit my friends head-on. My friends died; the two drunks lived. Why?

In a retreat I asked the group, "What is your most difficult problem relative to Christian Belief?" This was the answer of one woman:

> "Giving up all our children, whom we so much wanted and loved.
> First an infant son.
> Second an infant daughter.
> Third a daughter 13½ years old.
> There was no bitterness in my soul — but a deep heart hunger."

Why?

Walk down any street, in any city, in any country of the world. It's there, behind the doors and windows that line that street. In my congregation, a mother with three children is struck down by polio. Why? A useful woman doing an effective work with the youth of her church loses her eyesight. Why? A dedicated man, capable, involved, is destroyed by a heart attack. Why? A young Christian couple from our congregation rejoices over the birth of their first child. I meet them in the hospital hall. The doctor has just told them their child can never be a normal person. Why?

Why? Why? Why? Job flung it at heaven. And why wouldn't he? His false comforters had come to see him on the garbage heap. They had said, "It's simple, Job. You have sinned. Admit it. Repent and this will be lifted from you." Job knew it was not that simple. He knew he was not perfect. But he knew he loved God and tried to serve him. He knew there was a deeper reason.

Even though Job was "patient," he got fed-up with his cliche-speaking friends and declared, "I am sure that wisdom will die with you!"

Job continued his desperate quest: "O that I knew where I might find him, that I could lay my case before him." Job challenged God: "What's wrong? Where did I miss it? Is it my fault? What are you doing, God? Is there an answer? Just explain it to me, God." God doesn't mind confrontation. When we engage with him and he engages with us, we begin to work things out. Rather than assertiveness, it's indifference that separates us from God, and from discovery.

If this world, this experience of life, were all there was, then we might assume that justice does not prevail. It takes God two worlds to complete his process of justice. He planned it that way. Christ makes it clear that there is another life where the process of fulfillment is completed. Someone put it aptly: "The dawn of another world breaks upon this world's sorrow." I believe it. I also believe that our Heavenly Father is seeking to heal our hurts here as well as hereafter.

Carl Michaelson was a brillant young theologian who lost his life in an air crash almost twenty years ago. In one of his books he tells of a revealing incident. He and his little son were playing on the lawn, roughing it up, as father and son will do. In the play Carl's elbow hit the little fellow on the head. It hurt. His son was about to cry. Before he did, he looked up into his father's eyes. There he saw, not anger, but only love and sorrow that he had accidentally hurt his son. Instead of crying, the little fellow broke out laughing. It made all the difference in the world, what he saw in his father's eyes.

There is a great truth here. What do you see in your Heavenly Father's eyes when you hurt? That's where trust comes in. On a cross Christ looked up into his Father's eyes. He was content. He whispered, "Into thy hands I commend my spirit."

Job, in his agony, looked up into the eyes of God. There he caught a glimpse of love, and something deep within him cried out, "I know that my Redeemer liveth." God is working something out. All this will make sense some day. My Father loves me.

An angry mother came to Paul Scherer. She flung at him this question: "Where was God when my son was killed?" Of course she was bitter because of her son's accident. Dr. Scherer, a wise and compassionate pastor, answered with divine insight: "I don't know, I don't know, unless he was where he was when his son was killed." God aware. God caring. God, himself, entering this world's sorrow. God involved in my anguish. God suffering with Christ and with all his children in the redemptive process. You know, we can best see the eyes of God when we look into the eyes of Christ. There is no doubt what we see there.

We pursue the mystery, and we glimpse meaning. You remember the young couple whose first-born child could not be a normal person. Their faith amazed me. They were calm; they revealed a depth of faith I did not expect. Ten years later I visited my old parish. This was a happy, loving family. Two lovely, normal children had been born to them. The whole family loved the retarded child with a beautiful compassion. This family had become the leaders in the work among the retarded children of this community. I do not for a moment think that God caused the child to be retarded. But God was present in love and compassion. He got through to those parents, and they became a blessing to others.

Just recently I saw this courageous family. They told me that the retarded child, now near twenty years of age, had just passed away. I could tell them with all the confidence of my faith that their son was now with God, now in full life with all his capacities in full strength, now fully alive for the first time. This beautiful couple saw something in the eyes of God, and their lives reflected what they saw. I trust this world because God is in it; I trust the next world because God is there. The two worlds are inseparable.

Suffering can be a spur to the *conquering* of suffering. Our children lived under the terrible threat of polio. Our grandchildren have no fear of this disease. The terrible onslaught of polio a generation ago drove men like Dr. Salk and others into persistent research until polio was conquered. Diphtheria, smallpox, and many similar threats to life have thus been overcome. A throng of men and women, now driven by the threat of cancer and heart disease, will eventually find the answer. And a loving God is with them in the process.

I am told that six out of seven of the world's great leaders have suffered intensely. Perhaps the conquest of suffering is an ingredient of greatness. At any rate, suffering can be the pressure chamber in which the spirit is conditioned for the next stage of life. Once a successful businessman in my congregation was struck down by a very serious illness. Before his sickness, he was hard-boiled, selfish, and unaware. He cared little for anyone but himself. He suffered intensely for months. I visited him regularly in the hospital and always had a brief prayer at the end of the visit.

One day I was surprised at a new reaction. He asked, "How is Mr. Jones down the hall?" (Before this he had been unaware of others.) The strange process of change continued. He would ask, "How are the men who work for me?" On and on it went as his concern for others grew. It was beautiful. His attitude toward life was different; his values were new.

He died. But before he died he had become ready to live, really live. And when you are ready to live, you are ready to die. The *reality* of life is the same on both sides of death. As someone has put it, "It is not that we can't find God; the truth is we can't get rid of him." He pursues us in love.

Let's get one thing straight: suffering is not to be enjoyed. You do not lie down and let it run over you. You fight against suffering and all shapes of evil. Jesus fought it victoriously every day of his ministry. Science fights it; God fights it. Suffering may be a kind of tunnel you pass through to get to higher ground, like a pass in the Alps. There the vista of life opens up and the air is clear. "You can see forever." There is the wholesome elation of altitude. The tunnel itself is not pleasant. It is dark, smoky, dusty, gloomy; you do not want to settle down and live there. You seek and strive to pass through to the next stage in life, whatever that is for you.

Now let's return to our friend Job. What's become of him by this time? In agony he catches a glimpse of the face of God — several glimpses. (Often God speaks to us in our own words.) Job heard himself saying, "Though he slay me, yet will I trust him." No matter what happens, though life defeat me, though illness take my powers, though accident bring me disability, though loss leave me in loneliness, yet will I trust Life and God who is back of life. I will trust the Wisdom within and above all life, the Goodness undergirding life, the Love that flavors and fulfills life. In suffering Job had caught a glimpse of the eyes of God.

Still all this is a mystery. A doctor reminds me that if he had been there, and had penicillin been available, he would have given Job a shot of penicillin. He would have cured Job quickly. It would have been a sin not to have treated him. But the doctor continued, "What a loss! Humanity would never have gotten this insight into suffering." Such is the unresolved mystery of life!

But the clear glimpses of meaning continue to appear. As we put it together, the facts of existence begin to emerge. God wills goodness; he wills health; he wills joy; he wills life. Varied forms of evil, again and again, break in upon life. God works against all evil and calls us to do the same. The struggle can be used in the fulfillment of life. Suffering can be redemptive. Not all suffering is redemptive; at times, we won't let it be.

In the midst of our suffering, glimpses of light and understanding break through. God speaks between the lines of our sorrow. He doesn't give answers in five or six simple words. Nor do we really want this. We don't want God speaking in worn-out cliches. We need to have him grapple with our sorrow in a way more meaningful, more involved than that. Flashes of light penetrate our darkness. A new grasp of truth is given.

Listen to Job talking to himself. It is God speaking to Job as well: "I know that my Redeemer liveth." Hope flashes from the eyes of God. This is not the end. God will not let you down. We will not ultimately be destroyed. Job was beginning to grasp that Life somehow, somewhere, does make sense.

Let John speak from exile, as he catches a glimpse of the eyes of God: "I saw a New Heaven and a New Earth coming down from God out of heaven and I heard a great voice saying, 'Behold, God shall be their God, and they shall be his people and there shall be no more death, no more sorrow, no more crying. For the former things are passed away. Everything has been made fresh and new!' "

Paul, looking into the eyes of God, cries out: "Who can separate us from the love of Christ? Can tribulation, peril or sword? Can life or death, things present or things to come? No! *In all these things* we are more than conquerors through him that loved us."

God is holding us in his concern. He seeks to use each situation to lift us closer to himself, closer to the fulfillment of our lives. No matter how deep the mystery, God acts in love. All things *do* work together for good to those who have seen the eyes of God in the eyes of Christ and have learned to trust him.

Job had been fitted by calamity; he had been instructed by pain; he had been educated by loneliness; he had been purified by suffering; he had glimpsed what lay beyond the shadows; and he might have declared:

"The world's no blank for me, no blot. It means intensely, and it means God!" When all else is said and done, God is still good -- and so is what he is doing in his world."

Job's last condition, they say, was better than his first. It is not so much, however, that he regained what he had lost. He had entered into a new dimension of life. Listen to the new Job: "I had heard of thee by hearing of the ear, but now mine eye seeth thee."

To know God is life's ultimate answer! Like Job, you and I first may discover for ourselves life's meaning. We can know it first-hand, not merely by rumor or hearsay — for God bids us look into his eyes, to see the love and suffering there.

> God's dream for us
> Far past our comprehension;
> Toward Destiny
> God strains with us
> Along the way!

What do you see in God's eyes when you hurt?

6

Coping When It Seems Impossible

No problem! No sweat! My life is under control. My family is under control. My business is under control. My Nation is under control. My world is under control. No sweat!

How stupid can we get? Help! I need help!

Our world is not coping well. We tremble on the brink of suicide. Self-trust dismisses God's authority. In some cases entire nations fail the most fundamental test of helping their own citizens cope with materialism run amok. Perhaps the most complete expression of a totally materialistic philosophy in control and in action is Russian Communism. But Russians are a hungry people, searching for more than their government provides. Twenty years ago I was a member of a study group sent to Russia by the Methodist Board of Social Concerns. There were thirty of us in the group: doctors, teachers, agriculturists, pastors, professors. We were seeking the foundations of peace. It was a fascinating experience.

Our guides were brilliant young Communists, working their way up in the party. Born since the Revolution, they knew nothing of Christianity. Yet, they were curious and watched us, a group of Christians, with searching attention. Simultaneously, they lost no opportunity to emphasize the fact that they did not believe in God. A group of children would cross in front of the bus. Our guide would point out, "They are Young Pioneers; they are like your Boy Scouts, but *they don't believe in God — they don't believe in God.*"

After having spent three weeks visiting all over Russia, experiencing nearly all areas of Russian life, we found ourselves on our last Sunday in Tashkent, near the border of China. It was a dry, near-desert, country. We told our guides we wanted to go out into the desert to worship. They replied: "This is em-poss-ible." We insisted. They took us.

When one lives three weeks in an officially atheistic culture, faith takes on new meaning. We deeply felt our faith and sensed its reality. One of us, with deep feeling, read from the New Testament. Our guides had never heard it read before. One of us prayed, talking fervently to our Father in heaven. This was probably our guides' first prayer experience. Then we sang, from memory, some of the old Christian hymns. It was singing from our hearts, speaking of our hunger and our faith. The singing, too, was new to them. Finally, one of us gave a brief meditation on our Christian faith and what it meant to us. There were tears in the eyes of one of our guides.

The next day we took a long trip in a very noisy bus. One of our guides came and sat by me. She began asking questions about Christianity. I thought she wanted to argue; but soon I discovered that, out of her repressed spiritual hunger, she really wanted to know. A child of God, deprived of the reality of faith, wanted answers that only faith can give. She had seen friends and loved ones die. She was told, "There is nothing more: they are dead!" But she wondered about the mystery of death: could there be more? She had made mistakes; she needed some sense of forgiveness. She was told that there was nothing there, no one to forgive. Go try harder! they would urge her. But she wondered. She struggled with these and other basic human questions which were not answered by her dialectical philosophy. She was comforted to discover that Christianity really dealt with these questions of faith and found deep answers in experience.

The old bus reached its destination. The motor was stopped, and in the dangerous silence she could ask no more questions. As she arose to go, she bent over and whispered, "I want to thank you. This has met a deep need in my life." This young woman had found new hope for coping with life, coping which is quite impossible without faith in a universe that has purpose and direction, and without faith in a God who loves us and is able to see us through.

Russia is spiritually sensitive. Russia is spiritually starved. The next great Spiritual Awakening can happen in Russia and may run like wild fire. Not only could this feed and satisfy individual hungers, it could heal dangerous world tensions (if it were also matched by a genuine spiritual awakening in the West).

Recently I read a statement which I believe is a glimpse of basic truth. It declared that the Age of Secularism had come to an end, because this philosophy was not answering life's ultimate problems. The declaration continued that A New Age of the Spirit had begun. If this is true, and I believe it is, then, in the perspective of faith, we had better look again at our personal lives, our human relationships, and our world tensions. If we are ready, God just might step in again. Then, beyond just focusing on ways of coping, we would discover an ultimate direction and a sustaining strength.

Last autumn, while preaching for two months in Johannesburg, South Africa, I visited in a home in Durban. During the year this couple had lost their only son in a motorbike accident. He had just been graduated from the University and had faced a bright future. We talked until midnight and discovered that they had been able to cope with this tragedy only by a rediscovery of a vital faith. They had been amazingly sustained and were growing into beautiful people who were helping other tragedy-ridden people to find the faith that heals, that sustains, and that points to a future of victory.

Recently I was preaching in St. Austell in South West England. By chance a minister on holiday from another part of England worshiped with us. We felt God present with us in the service. Afterwards this visiting pastor came forward and told me of great tension in his local congregation and community. He said that he was about to break under the load. He confided that it was providential that he had been present, for he was going back to his congregation with new confidence and the power of love renewed. There is power available for life and its demands. "The vast resources of his power open to us who trust him." (Ephesians 1:18)

When God calls us to something, he sustains us in it. You can count on that. Read through the New Testament book of Acts and see how God backs up his promise under impossible odds. There is then, for us a steady inner peace available as we face a needy and broken world, seeking to do God's will as interpreted by Christ.

One evening at a dialogue dinner of pastors and psychiatrists, the doctor sitting next to me thought to shock me. He said, "Pastor, this morning there was a woman in my office beside herself with guilt. She would not be quieted. I said to her, 'Forget it! No good God is going to send one of his children to hell.' "

"You are right, Doctor," I answered. "God is not in the business of sending his children to hell, but of getting them out of hell. For this he sent Christ into the world, for this he allowed the suffering of the

Cross. People put *themselves* in hell; God seeks to save them from their lostness.

"But Doctor," I continued, "this morning you saw a woman in hell, by her own conscious or unconscious decisions, separated from God, separated from love and peace, separated from meaningful life. If she continues in this state of willful separation and dies in it, she is in hell. But God does not want it so. If she can accept the love and forgiveness of Christ, she will be free, and she will *know* she is free. God will even go the second mile to help her."

My sister taught in one of our United Methodist Colleges. She was a person of love and generosity. She was a means of strength to many students. She gave unselfishly, and alone built a small church in India. But she had intellectual problems and theological uncertainties. She died at age fifty. Just before she died she said to her sister, "I never have been able to understand it all, but I have loved Christ and loved people; and now I see that even though there are things I cannot completely grasp, somehow *Christ makes up the difference.*" She died at peace, her life complete.

A few years ago, I worked very closely with a psychiatrist in our community. I referred patients to him whom I thought needed deeper psychological treatment than I could give. On occasion he would send me a patient whom he felt needed more specific spiritual care. One case I shall never forget. She was a young mother who had completely gone to pieces. I can see her now as she sat across the office from me. Wringing her hands in abject agony, she cried out: "I can't trust God. I can't trust God." She had lost hold on life, on her husband, on her children. How do you help a person, so desperate, to come to grips with life? When we are inwardly prayerful, God guides in our counseling. I said, "Well, if you can't trust God, he is not mad at you. He is concerned about you; he is worried about one of his children who is all mixed up and suffering. He cares." Then another thought was given me. Knowing that she had some Christian background, I asked, "If you had lived in the time of Christ, if you had followed the multitudes of needy, sick people who followed him, if you had heard him speak, if you had seen him heal all kinds of people, if you had seen him forgive people broken in sin, if you had seen him pick up the little children in his arms, would you have trusted *him*? Would you have said in your heart, 'This is someone who would not lead anyone into a blind alley. This is one who would not let you down'? Could you have trusted Jesus?"

A little light came into her face. And she said hesitantly, "Yes, I believe I could have trusted Jesus." I replied, "If you could have trusted Jesus, might you not trust the Father in heaven who gave us Jesus, who is back of Jesus, who shows us his love in Jesus?" Again, her reply was hesitantly positive. We had a prayer. She had started back into life. In a few weeks she was once more a normal person. She had found her faith again, and she could cope with the responsibilities that had been crushing her.

One of the great needs in life is being able to resist temptation. The call of the lesser life, the break with reality, can at times get a death hold upon us. Dr. Charles McKay, former President of Princeton Seminary, was, in his younger days, a missionary to Brazil. I heard him tell this story:

A young man in his little mission church on the edge of the Brazilian jungle had a real conversion to Christ. Formerly he had been a member of a rough robber gang. After conversion he totally broke with the old group.

Then one day the old gang showed up in the yard of his little cabin. They wanted him to join them for just one more job, a big one. His frightened wife watched from the little porch. She saw them beg, and John refuse. She saw them threaten, and John stand firm. Then she saw them call him a coward, say that he was yellow. She now saw John clench his fists, she saw the color come to his face, and she saw the veins swell in his neck. In desperation she cried out, "Remember Christ, John. Remember Christ!" Normal color returned to his cheeks, she saw his fists released, and the veins of his neck become relaxed. John took it. Under the sway of Christ, he took it.

We can handle life, when we do not try to handle it alone. It helps to remember that Christ faced everything we have to face. He side-stepped nothing.

With faith there comes a subconscious surge of energy to do the necessary thing. Faith is directed by prayer to specific needs. Through faith, specific prayer channels its energies directly to particular situations.

Our universe has judgment built into it. God made it so. We can depend on its structure. Build a building by the plumb line and it will stand. Fail to do so and it will fall. Build a life on integrity and it will stand. Fail to do so and it crashes about you. Build a business on honesty and it prospers. Fail to do so and it comes apart. Build a home on fidelity and real love and it endures. Fail in this and there is separation and sorrow. Build a nation on righteousness and it can lead the world. Build it on aggression, selfishness and no moral commitment and it will fall, dragging other nations down with it.

Into such a universe God sent Christ to forgive us for the times we have broken with the structure of reality. Furthermore, God gives us Christ to enable us to move constructively within the limits of reality. Christ forgives our sins, and also sustains us in our struggle with life's great demands. Faith in Christ releases enabling energy and guidance.

Recently my son, who is a seminary professor in the Midwest, had a young doctor come to him. The doctor said, "Tuttle, I have everything I've ever wanted. My practice is excellent. I have all the money I need. I have two cars and a lovely home. I have a wonderful wife and three beautiful children. Why do I want to blow my brains out?"

"It seems that all this has been your God," my son replied, "You've achieved all your goals. You've lived your life. It's over. But before you end it all, I want you to try one thing. Turn the whole thing over to God: your practice, your self, your wealth, your home, your family. From now on, work not for yourself but for God. He has something great in mind for you. You will not just be fixing up sick bodies, you will be ministering to sick, frightened people, making them whole in body and spirit, by your medical skills and by the power of God's love. You will never catch up, because God will lead you into new levels of healing and ministry. You will be thrilled by what you see in your patients' faces. You will thank God daily for new life and joy. When we risk the whole business on God, it becomes then not merely a matter of coping: there will result a whole new surge of life and purpose."

The young doctor got the message and, in his desperation, took the dare. Now he has entered a glorious new phase of medicine. The Cross became for him a practical life principle.

There is Hope in the Cross —
    Hope for me!
God's Agony on a Cross;
God's Presence in Earth's Darkness.

There is Hope in the Cross —
    Hope for me!

God's Victory beyond the Cross;
God's Light, God's Life;
God's Presence in the Eternal.

There is Hope in the Cross —
    Hope for me!
God's head bowed down
God's arms outstretched
God's heart accepting me —
    Even me!

We have a God who knows the meaning of suffering, a God who has borne a cross himself. Here is a portion of a letter I received recently from a former parishioner who is obviously suffering from deep depression:

"I am writing this letter to keep from going insane!
Every morning I wake up moaning and groaning!
I want to run away! But I am not even able to dress and pack,
    and I would never be able to get my belongings together.
But I'd rather die than live out the rest of my life here.
Actually I *am* dead. I can't function here! I can't even hardly
    wash my hair or take a bath! I dread washing my hair.
It is so quiet here I want to scream.
If only I had some money and somewhere to go.
I am so disorganized and disoriented . . . I am so sick!

This person seems to have more than her share of problems, both inner and outer. She has had counseling without great success. I believe that lithium, properly administered, might change the picture for her.

I have recently completed reading a book by Ronald A. Fieve entitled *Moodswing*. It is a very interesting study on depression, its highs and lows. Dr. Fieve quotes a patient:

"My lows started 15 years ago, when I started to be afraid of things in my business that had never bothered me before. I was afraid to give orders. I was afraid to reprimand an employee. I was afraid to be criticized by my superiors. I was afraid to get up in the morning to face my store. I was afraid to go to sleep. I couldn't sleep nights. I couldn't taste my food. I would go to work and then turn around and go home . . .

After being on lithium for five years it was like a new world in front of me. I enjoyed my work so much. I looked forward to the mornings so I could be at my store. I made decisions fast and right."

Dr. Fieve uses the Lithium-Carbonate treatment very effectively. But he warns against its dangers and makes it clear that the lithium level in a patient must be monitored constantly. Some sufferers from depression need to have a vital chemical balance restored; some need to be loved, and to discover a trust that will let their own body systems bring about healing. Christ knew that moodswings were often symptomatic of a deeper need for wholeness. He healed desperate people then, and still does.

All of us have problems. In every generation people do. One of life's purposes is to solve problems, both personal and social. That is how we grow and become real persons. The apostle Paul saw this with precise clarity: "I have learned to find resources in myself whatever my circumstances. I know what it is to be brought low, and I know what it is to have plenty. I have very thoroughly been initiated into the human lot with all its ups and downs — fullness and hunger, plenty and want. *I have strength for anything through him who gives me power.*"

If we could share the faith of Paul, most of us would have no problem coping. Christ is an enabling Christ. But persons caught in the pressures of our secularized civilization go on from "burn-out" to "burn-out," and finally collapse. Christ came to change all this. And the Holy Spirit groans with us and for us "with groanings which cannot be uttered."

This power to heal and enable can be put in another way:

> It was a naive but impressive tribute . . . when Kenny Everett said about the "Peter Pan Christian," Cliff Richard, "I don't know what he's on, but it works!" (Derick Greeves, Expository Times)

I know what Paul "was on," and it works!

Behind Paul, we "look at that man on the cross and realize that behind the universe there is not a God who destroys the world but rather One who comes into it to reach out and try to make us healthy, to save us, to give us hope to keep going, who helps calm the storms and floods of our lives." (Dr. Henry Sawatzky)

There is infinite comfort in a verse by Ernesto Cardenal:

> When the siren wails the last warning
> You will be with me.
> You will be my refuge
> My strength and deep shelter.

It is strength to know that "every child of God can defeat the world."

A new Army recruit from my church was thrust suddenly into the cold, dark, arctic night in Thule, Greenland. From there he wrote me a letter: "Pastor, last night as I lay on my bunk in the dark, suddenly I saw how good God has been to me, how hard he has worked for me, how much he has done for me. Pastor, how can I pay him back?"

He had begun to answer his own question. He had discovered the source of his origin, his life, his guidance, his strength, his mission, his joy and his peace, and ultimately his destiny. He had glimpsed the Eternal.

The old hymn by John Neale throws out the challenge to all of us who struggle with the limitations of our human-ness.

> Art thou weary,
> Art thou troubled,
> Art thou sore distressed?
> "Come to me," saith One,
> "And coming, be at rest."

Bruce Larson, in a recent book,* says, "Doctors have been telling me for years that "You can't kill a happy man." He continues, "Happy people rarely get sick and tend to recover quickly when they do get sick. The unhappy person is the target for any and every kind of illness." Larson goes on to share the secret of his ability to cope with life: "We Christians, of all people, have a good reason to hope. Hope is a gift of God based on the belief that God created us and is

---

*Bruce Larson, *There's a Lot More to Health Than Not Being Sick*, 1981, Word Books, Waco, Texas.

our friend and helper. If I believe in a God who cares about me and enters into my life, then my future is truly unlimited. If I am an accident of creation or a biological mistake, then I have no reason to think that I will be anything other than what I have always been. If I am God's child, *I can get my act together* and begin to reverse what up to now may have been an unproductive and unpromising record."

Paul Tournier, who learned to cope with life and has taught thousands of others the secret of coping, writes: "Our attitude to life is always a reflection of our attitude to God. Saying 'yes' to God is saying 'yes' to life, to all its problems and difficulties." Tournier goes on to say, "God wills the development of all men. When from time to time he makes them hear his call to self-denial, to renunciation and even self-sacrifice, it is not for their impoverishment but for their enrichment."*

Leslie D. Weatherhead, the great English preacher of the last generation, describes a difficult incident in the life of a pastor and his secret of coping: He had come home from a difficult meeting, tired and disappointed. He dropped into his chair with deep bitterness in his blood. He wanted to write a letter to crush his opponent. Destructive and mean phrases began to form in his mind. He tried to pray, but didn't really want to. He then tried an experiment: he relaxed in body and mind, and left the door of his mind swinging open. There was "a vague longing for the coming of the Friend," the Friend who understands, even when we are upset and not ourselves. It happened. The peace that passes understanding flooded his whole being, his mind. His mind was quieted. He didn't see a Vision or hear a Voice, but the last thing he wanted to do at that moment was to write that destructive letter. To put it in Dr. Weatherhead's own words, "There is only one explanation of such an experience. God's greatest gift to man was given and accepted. The Friend came."**

Christ is in the garden. The disciples are asleep. He struggles alone. "Let this cup pass. Nevertheless Thy will be done." Will we ever have to face more than he has faced? The Father answered. Christ arose and faced the Roman soldiers. He stood his false trial with grand dignity. He endured the Cross, and completed his journey, whispering, "Father into thy hands I commend my spirit."

With Christ, I can handle anything I have to face; in the strength of Christ, I can cope.

*Paul Tournier. *Reflections*. Harper & Row, 1976, p. 109.
**Leslie D. Weatherhead. *The Transforming Friendship*, Abingdon Press, 1931, p. 28.

7

Christ and Healing

Jesus' ministry was one of healing. He said, "I came to minister to the sick and not the well." He never refused or failed to heal anyone who came to him in need.

There is no doubt about it: Christ constantly performed miracles of healing. His miracles were all tied in with love and forgiveness and produced whole persons in a new relationship with God and with life.

J. B. Phillips, in one of his last books, shares his own understanding of the miracles of Jesus. He says that these miracles are revealed glimpses into ultimate reality. The miracles of healing declare that there is no sickness in heaven. The healing miracles of Jesus are relevations of the ultimate health created by God's love and power, breaking in upon the incomplete present world.

Here is one day in the life of Jesus as recorded in Matthew, Chapter Nine (NEB):

"Even as he spoke, there came a president of the synagogue, who bowed low before him and said, 'My daughter has just died; but come and lay your hand on her, and she will live.' Jesus rose and went with him, and so did his disciples.

"Then a woman (as he was on his way) who had suffered from hemorrhages for twelve years came up from behind, and touched the edge of his cloak; for she said to herself, 'If I can only touch his cloak, I shall be cured.' But Jesus turned and saw her, and said, 'Take heart, my daughter, your faith has cured you.' And from that moment she recovered.

"When Jesus arrived at the president's house and saw the flute-players and the general commotion, he said, 'Be off! The girl is not dead: she is asleep;' but they only laughed at him. But, when everyone had been turned out, he went into the room and took the girl by the hand, and she got up. This story became the talk of all the country round.

"As he passed on Jesus was followed by two blind men, who cried out, 'Son of David, have pity on us!' And when he had gone indoors they came to him. Jesus asked, 'Do you believe that I have the power to do what you want?' 'Yes, Sir,' they said. Then he touched their eyes, and said, 'As you have believed, so let it be'; and their sight was restored. Jesus said to them sternly, 'See that no man hears about this.' But as soon as they had gone out they talked about him all over the country-side.

"They were on their way out when a man was brought to him, who was dumb and possessed by a devil; the devil was cast out and the patient recovered his speech. Filled with amazement the onlookers said, 'Nothing like this has ever been seen in Israel.' "

One day! I am out of breath! And all I did was to retell the story! The Power expressed in the presence of Jesus is almost unbelievable. But he still has that power; and he is still present with us.

A witness recently given by a minister in the North Carolina *Christian Advocate* shows just how clear the presence of Christ can be today: "In the wee hours of the morning (after neuro-surgery) on July 13, while still in the N.S.U. with all other patients apparently asleep, the door of that unit opened. In that door stood the Great Physician. Not one word was spoken. When he turned to leave he gave an above-the-shoulder signal indicating to me that 'all is well' . . .

"Before the night was gone I became aware that he had by his miraculous means set a bit of malignancy that had had to be left (in surgery), or suffer brain damage, so that it could be attacked by radiation.

"When morning came my wife came for her visit. Before entering the room she asked about my condition and how the night had gone. The nurse replied that I had had a good night, but that I had had a Visitor — The Great Physician — and that I had talked with her about it . . .

"I am not sure of the date, but probably that very day, I was carried for a C.A.T. scan — the very machine that had found the tumor. A couple of days later Dr. Gang came to my room to report his findings. He had the appearance of the most grateful surgeon with whom I have been in any way associated. He told the story with eyes beaming and almost streaming. He had removed a malignant tumor, but had had to leave a tiny bit of the malignancy, but according to the scan it was at a place that could be attacked by radiation. The very thing that I knew from the Great Physician's visit . . .

"In late September after twenty-eight radiation treatments, I returned to my pulpit. An examination in May of this year showed no recurrence."

I know this man. His witness stands.

Once, when I was threatened by almost certain death, I was praying desperately. The words of Jesus in a healing incident came to me: The sick man had said, "Master, if you will, you can make me whole." The Master answered, "I will." And the man was healed. In my mind, as I prayed, I heard the whisper, "I will." My fear was gone. My mind was at peace. I went through surgery with complete assurance and came out whole. Something happened in that prayer. I was in touch; he was in touch. He is present in today's world.

A few years ago, I was preaching in a mission in Adelaide, Australia. This story came to me concerning the pastor with whom I was working. He had suffered a devastating heart attack. He had undergone surgery. He had returned home, but he couldn't get well. His body just would not function. He was in dark despair. Well past midnight one morning, lying there in bed, he was about to give up. Then quietly there came to him the passage in James, Chapter Five: "Is one of you ill? He should send for the elders of the congregation to pray over him and anoint him with oil in the name of the Lord. The prayer offered in faith will heal the sick man, the Lord will raise him from his bed . . . "

My friend was caught up in this declaration. At three AM he called up the leader of the elders of his church. He said, "Jim, I have just read this passage from James. I want you to come over right away and pray for me." The elder replied, "Pastor, I have never done this. I have no special power; you are the Man of Prayer." But the Pastor would not take "No!" for an answer. He said, "Jim, I am dying. You have got to come."

The elder arrived. He laid hands on his pastor and prayed. His pastor was healed and soon returned to his church. The Pastor and his elder were so impressed by this experience of the presence of Christ that they shared it with the congregation. And the whole church was caught up in new life. I experienced this when I was there working with them. There was a special Spirit and a Power at work in that church and through that church.

I share a personal experience: An outstanding leader in our church, a Ph.D. in engineering and a vice-president of his corporation, had a near-fatal heart attack. He was rushed to a Cardiac Care Unit in a hospital thirty miles away. I hurried over to see him. The doctors were holding out little hope for his survival. I went into the Cardiac Unit, held his hand and said just a brief prayer of faith and hope. I left to return the next morning. As I walked down the hall, inwardly I caught a glimpse of Christ standing at the foot of his bed. I felt, in that experience, that my friend was going to make it. He felt the experience of Presence so deeply he has never forgotten it. He is still growing in his experience of Christ.

Once, while recuperating from surgery in a large hospital, I felt most deeply the Presence of Christ as I walked up and down the hall and talked with other patients. I could see that they felt a power and a peace. At times we Christians are permitted to be that healing Presence of Christ to other people. This is one specific dimension of Christianity coming alive today.

I am excited by a recent article in the *Readers Digest*, "Thoughts of a Brain Surgeon," by Robert J. White, M.D. The article reveals a beautiful blending of faith and technical skills. Dr. White, a renowned neurosurgeon, tells of a lovely little six-year-old girl. As he operated on her for a large brain tumor, "suddenly the hemisphere collapsed and the large vessels on its surface ruptured, flooding my operating field with blood.

"My colleagues and I struggled to stem the torential flow, but we were losing the battle . . . With my fingers, I held little pads of cotton tight against the hemorrhaging vessels . . . I dared not release my fingers. All I could do was pray while the child was transfused . . .

"No one, including me, believed I could lift my fingers from the pressure points without releasing another river of blood. I kept applying digital pressure and praying, praying to God to will the necessary strength into my hands.

"And then, quite suddenly, I felt relaxed. I knew I had done all that was in my power to do, and I was full of the comfortable certainty that I could proceed. Somehow God was in the room with us. Carefully, slowly, I released my pressure on the vessels, one finger at a time. There was no bleeding until all my fingers were free. Then one vessel began to bleed, but it was easily controlled.

"It took 4½ hours to remove the tumor . . . Her wounds healed well: no re-hemorrhaging, no neurological deficit, no brain damage . . . the girl today is a normal, happy teenager . . .

"For me, the practice of medicine and religious faith are inextricably interwoven. I pray a great deal, especially before and after surgery. I find prayer satisfying. I feel there are immense resources behind me, resources I need and want."

I think this is what Christ wants today in the field of healing, medical skills used with faith and love. This is why Oral Roberts' "City of Faith" interests me. Young doctors and nurses from all over the world will be trained there in the best of medical skills, plus a vital faith in Christ, plus a ministry of love and compassion. This is the healing climate needed in hospitals everywhere. God's love is shown especially in the ministry of healing.

"How is your wife?" I asked one of my members, as I met him in the hall of a large city hospital. He replied that she was desperately ill and that I had better not see her that night.

This woman's brilliant, talented daughter had died five or six years before. The mother had become bitter, and seemed to hate God and hate life. In her deeply disturbed emotional state a malignancy had taken over, and she was dying.

Entering her room the next morning, I could feel the tension and despair. The conversation was not satisfactory. Before leaving I had a brief prayer. I was guided to pray: "Father, give a quiet peace to this friend who is sick. We know she loved her daughter deeply. Let her know that Christine is now with you, that she is alive and happy, continuing the fulfillment of her life. Father, we believe that Christine is worried about her mother, especially since her sorrow is bringing this desperate illness. Let her know that Christine so wants her mother to be free, joyful, and well again. Grant this healing peace, Lord. Amen."

As I turned to go, she raised up in bed and almost shouted at me, "Do you believe that?" "Yes, I believe that," I answered, and left.

On my next visit, I noticed that she was a different person. She was radiant, alive, totally different. Soon she was at home, and shortly after that at work again. After going back to work she came by my study and said, "I guess you would like to know what happened to me." "Yes, very much," I said.

"Well," she continued, "after you left the hospital that day, I may have dozed off, I don't know. But there was Christine standing by my bed, lovely and very much alive. She told me how much she loved me and how concerned she was about my health. I have never seen her more alive. We had a marvelous visit. And then she was gone. But I know she is alive!"

My friend lived for several years as a beautiful, complete, caring person. She was always radiant, loving, and full of life. Something had happened. Through experience she had discovered faith. She *knew*. She was sure. She was alive again. Christ is just that near to us all the time. Sometimes it takes a special experience to open our eyes.

One of the truly outstanding psychiatrists of this nation told me a fascinating story. He had reached the top of his profession. His goals had been achieved. Frustration was setting in. Things were not so good at home. Desperate, he tried to get away from it all by taking a canoe trip into the wilderness of Canada.

It had rained all day. There was water, water everywhere, above, below, and all around. It was not a good environment for depression. His group pulled their canoes up on a rocky island for the night. The trees were dripping; the rocks were wet; the ground was soggy. My friend collapsed on a rock. He didn't feel like making camp. Why should he go on?

Something happened! Just at sunset there came a break in the clouds, a narrow slit of blue sky just above the horizon in the west. The sun broke through, clear, unpolluted. It swept the whole drowning earth with golden light and beauty. The drenched horizon was renewed. It was a different world. But that is not all. The sun, or the Power and Love back of the sun, broke in upon my friend's life and awareness in a way that cannot be explained. New life, new hope, new joy, new adequacy, new power, new peace flooded into him. Life had begun again; God had moved in.

Since that experience he has been a new man, a new psychiatrist, a new husband, a new father. A new dynamic has entered his ministry of healing. Everyone notices it. He tells me that before this religious experience he had had little success working with alcoholics and drug addicts. Now there is a more effective healing power. He *knows* something. There is something far beyond him that reaches out through him in his healing ministry. He is no more and no less a skilled psychiatrist than he had been before. But he is now an *inspired* psychiatrist. Christ is alive in his ministry of healing. It is that *plus* that holds the universe together; it is that everlasting love; it is that glimpse of the Eternal breaking through into this world's shadow. Thank God for an authentic witness like this man, ministering in one of our leading medical schools.

The healing power of Christ is expressed today in many and varied ways. In the May 7, 1980, issue of *The Christian Century*, a remarkable story is told by a brilliant young woman student of Duke University Divinity School. Even though she was suffering from cystic fibrosis, she was seeking to prepare herself for ministry to others. She died before she could graduate, but left an undying influence on her professors and fellow students.

At age twenty-two, she had only 39 percent lung capacity. With this disease one gradually smothers. She was exceptionally intelligent and had a long struggle justifying her illness over against a loving God. These are her words: "In my despair, I felt trapped alone in a howling darkness. I hated 'God.' " Beyond her struggle came experience. She began to see the meaning of Christ and the Cross: "God must know and care, after all, because he was in it with us."

She tells of this experience: "Suddenly there was a Presence in the room, a Person so alive that he almost made the air tingle, a Person who was utterly Good. He told me that what I had read was true, and that he loved me. The Person seemed to *be* Love, and Love (himself) was focused on me . . . I knew that . . . the I that I *was* would die, because it could never be the same again. I tried to resist, but it was useless, and so I surrendered myself, praying a humble prayer of confession of sin (for in this Person's presence I *knew* what love was, and how far short of it I had fallen in all ways).

"Immediately the darkness, hatred and despair in which I had been living were lifted away, leaving the Presence in my mind with me, almost like a traveling companion. And so I became a new creation in Christ Jesus."

After this she had some intellectual problems and some ups and downs of faith, but found her way back. "I remember Bonhoeffer's idea that faith and obedience are corollaries . . . (that) to recommit myself to God would be an act of *obedience*. I did so, went to bed, still speechless with distress, and woke up later, again *knowing* that my God is the loving father of the Lord Jesus Christ — he had restored my faith . . . Thus in six years as a Christian, I have come 360 degrees and am again faithful to the gospel I first received."

We too have our ups and downs. But Christ remains loyal to us in his love; and by *faith* and *obedience* we are whole again.

When he was healing others, Jesus was constantly saying, "You are well; go and sin no more." He knew that our personal break with God was responsible for much of our physical and mental breakdown. As a young pastor, I prayed fervently for a sick man in our church. He regained his health, but was just as ornery as before. I discovered that God wants healing of the whole person — body, mind, and spirit.

Healing prayers are not always answered the way we expect. I recall a preaching mission I conducted in another congregation. Toward the end of the week, the host pastor brought a couple to me after church one evening. They had a very sick child. They wanted me to pray for the child. We did. And I had a sense of answer. Therefore, I was greatly depressed when I returned home to discover that the child had died. I asked myself if I could really depend on that deep feeling that a prayer was being answered.

Then I received a letter from the parents of the child. The letter overflowed with joy and faith. They wrote that their little one was with God and that God had come into their home in a way they could never have expected. There was peace and assurance, faith and love on a deeper level. They felt close to their child and felt the very Presence of God. Their lives had been renewed. They wanted to thank me for the session of prayer. I was comforted. I saw that my prayer had been answered, but in a way I had not expected.

When I moved to the last congregation I served, a woman sick with cancer came to my office. She was overwhelmed with hate. Her family had mistreated her and she could not forgive them. So she went on hating and dying. Through several months of counseling she learned to forgive and to pray for the members of her family who had mistreated her. She relaxed, her health improved, and for several years she lived a very creative life. When she finally died, she died in love and faith (which is heaven), instead of hate and despair (which is hell).

Our next door neighbor, who lives alone, is fighting a battle with cancer. We pray for her constantly that she may realize the very Presence of Christ, his peace, his love, and the amazing eternal life that he offers. My wife and I seek to share with her Christian love and caring. We believe that she is discovering life in a dimension she has never known before. She is beginning to see the ultimate end of her life, and she is unafraid.

Christ is never absent. He is constantly at work in his world. He is at work through the presence of his Spirit, and at work through people in whom his Spirit expresses his love. Through *our* faith experience, we can make this Christ real to the struggling, frightened people of this sick world. Christ is still in the business of healing. We can partner with him, bringing hope and healing to a broken, hurting world. Be open, then, to God's gift of healing. While he may make us whole in ways we hadn't counted on, one thing is sure: he will not leave us in our brokenness.

Here is the true picture:

> Think not thou canst sigh a sigh
> And thy maker is not by;
> Think not thou canst weep a tear
> And thy maker is not near.
>
> He gives to us his joy,
> That our grief he may destroy;
> Till our grief is fled and gone
> He doth sit by us and moan.

> ("On Another's Sorrow" by William Blake)

8

Faith As Healing Energy

Most doctors would agree with Norman Cousins, who wrote recently in a national magazine, "The *belief system* is often activator of the *healing system*."* Faith actually affects the chemistry of the body. It can be so specific that it has been called "Spiritual energy injection." Faith makes a difference in health. Through faith (trust), energy channels are opened between the Creator and the created and our bodies begin to function as they are designed to.

Even when we feel as though we're cornered, we are never completely trapped. We are never totally imprisoned. There is always one side of the box left open. We can walk out. One side of our imprisonment always stands open — the side that opens toward God. Christ is the one who enables us to see that open door to health and abundant life.

"The belief system," continues Norman Cousins, "is a prime physiological reality. The greatest force in the human body is the natural drive of the body to heal itself — but that force is not independent of the belief system, which can translate expectations into physiological changes. Nothing is more wondrous about the 15 billion neurons in the human brain than their ability to convert thoughts, hopes, ideas, and attitudes into chemical substances. Everything begins, therefore, with belief. What we believe is the most powerful option of all."

Cousins insists that pain is not always an indication of poor health, but that "most frequently, it is the result of tension, stress, worry, idleness, boredom, frustration, suppressed rage," and

---

*Norman Cousins, *Saturday Evening Post*, April, 1982.

destructive habits. "If [people] can be programmed to die, they can be programmed to live."

Jesus always emphasized the necessity of faith: "O, ye of little faith!" "When the Son of Man comes will he find faith on earth?" "If you only had the faith of a mustard seed . . . nothing would prove impossible for you." How can the Father help you if you do not trust him?

Faith is reaching out toward "the real truth and the Supreme Reality . . . the *Good*, the supreme goal and the one and only Consummation of our life, the eternal, hidden and incomprehensible Peace." (Wilfred Cantwell Smith, *Faith and Belief*, Princeton Press) Faith bridges the gap between the contemporary and the eternal, between the present and the everlasting reality, between man and God. Smith says it well: faith is "opting out of a stream of history that [is] going nowhere, to plunge into and to be caught up in [the] surging movement" of the Kingdom of God. He goes on to tell us that "humankind is characterized by faith. The history of religion is the history of humanity. It has been so from paleolithic times to the present in every Continent, in every culture, in every age. Perhaps the modern West has in some way been an expectation."

We are the "Modern West." Where is our Faith? Where is our Assurance? Where is our Certainty? No wonder so many of us are sick! There is no realized certainty to unify our mental and physical functions. Emotionally we are disintegrating. No wonder our bodies are breaking down. We have been giving our "desires and whims priority over the truth," and nothing *real* sustains us.

Smith continues, "Standard man is a man of faith; and negative secularity is a strange and sometimes fierce asceticism directed against the spirit, which it can suppress but cannot eliminate." Faith "offers us the power to become what man was intended to be." Faith is "the essential human quality." "Faith is normal: but to abnormality man is naturally prone." And Christ weeps as he says to us, "O, ye of little faith."

One of the positive factors in health is the becoming aware of the "reserve brain power" and "Spirit power" waiting to be unlocked in us by faith. This is the rediscovery of the *transcendent* by Western Man. Thus, we follow Paul in realizing "the immense resources of God's power open to us who trust him."

Faith and hope are closely related. In fact, faith produces hope. Without faith there is very little real hope. Once while attending The

Oxford Institute, a periodic gathering of theologicans, teachers, and preachers at Oxford University, I heard an address given by a famous atheist, Dr. Francis Ayers, professor of Philosophy at Oxford. Dr. Ayers was an evangelistic atheist. It appeared that he wanted the whole world to be atheistic. He spoke brilliantly on the theme, "The Concept of God is Entirely Unnecessary for Moral and Ethical Living." He spoke with such impeccable logic that if I had started where he started I would have come out where he came out. But my presuppositions were quite different.

After speaking for an hour and a half, Dr. Ayers paused, took off his glasses, and looked at us. A new thought seemed to enter his mind. He said, almost in a whisper, "But I cannot compete with you. I have no hope." Imagine declaring one's life commitment so forcefully, and then admitting that it is no good. "I have no hope" is a devastating admission.

Look at Joni Eareckson. The summer of 1967, after she had graduated as "Most Athletic Girl" from a Baltimore high school, she broke her neck in a diving accident. As a result of this she is totally paralyzed from her neck down. It was not an optimistic picture. After waves of depression and searching, she discovered a deep and meaningful Christian faith. This faith has released in her a vitally creative life. She has become, in spite of her handicap, "a successful commercial artist, a bestselling author, and the star of a $2 million dollar film version of her life." (*Time*, Dec. 29, 1980).

Her spirit and her creative life are a miracle of faith. In one of her books, *A Step Further*, she writes: "If God's mind was small enough for me to understand, he wouldn't be God . . . Sometimes I can't stand being in a wheelchair, but there God's grace takes over. Even in my handicap, God has a plan and purpose for my life." She continues, "God began his earthly life in a stinky stable. He got angry. He was lonely. He went without a place to call his own, abandoned by his closest friends. He wept real tears. This is a God I can trust. I know my tears count with him."

As they were with Joni, faith and Christian fellowship are a healing power for all of us. Recently I had a phone call from a Korean business man. A year ago he was desperately ill with something like a ruptured disc. Over a period of months I visited him and prayed with him. He discovered not long ago that I had hurt my back. The call was to ask me how I was and to tell me that he had prayed for me. Strangely, about three days later, my back suddenly got better. I like to think that the prayer and the concern were a real part of the healing. Such a world of deep faith and compassionate caring for each other is the world that Christ wants us to establish. It is his Kingdom.

Perhaps it is not so much a miracle of healing that I need, but the miracle of a loving, believing fellowship which produces the miracle of healing. In his book, *There's A Lot More to Health Than Not Being Sick*, Bruce Larson tells us that a recent survey by the American Medical Association revealed that "by their estimate, 90 per cent of the people who see a general practitioner in an average week have no medically treatable problem. Certainly they are ill and suffering real pain, but their problem is not chemical or physical and defies normal medical procedure . . . Most of the doctors said they would like to have had time to spend an hour a week talking to these patients about their lives, their families, and their jobs."

Bruce Larson suggests that since the doctors do not have time to do this, the Church could become this listening, caring, believing, loving fellowship where many of these people could find healing. This is what Jesus did every day. Some small Christian fellowship groups are doing just that in today's world. Let the Church be the healing fellowship for today's brokenness.

The Christian minister could be the key person in this climate of faith, hope, and wholeness. Through his counseling, when he employs not only psychological skills, but his own special gift of faith and love, the *healing spirit of the universe* is evident in the minister's presence. It is felt by the counselee, and healing and growth take place.

Bruce Larson tells of a surgeon who says to a patient as he is dismissing her after a "face lift," "My dear, I have done an extraordinary job on your face, as you can see in the mirror. I have charged you a great deal of money, and you were happy to pay it. But I want to give you some free advice. Find a group of people who love God and who will love you enough to help you deal with the negative emotions inside of you. If you don't, you will be back in my office in a very short time with your face in far worse shape than before."

Negative emotions register, positive emotions register; both show through in our appearance and in our health. Teilhard de Chardin, the French priest and scientist, once wrote, "Joy is the surest sign of the presence of God." This joy that comes from the living experience of faith and love was very evident in a luncheon Prayer and Study Group which met every Wednesday in a church I once served. This group became a kind of "depressurization chamber" for those who were seeking to "return to life" from various traumatic experiences. Persons returning to the community from alcoholic rehabilitation or from mental hospitals, or from divorce, or from tragedy, found acceptance here until they found an inner strength sufficient to face the raw outer world from which they had retreated.

One case especially stands out in my memory. A young doctor's wife was concerned about a neighbor who was about to go to pieces over drugs and alcohol. The young wife brought the neighbor to the fellowship group whenever she would come. She brought her to my study for counseling. Apparently the woman couldn't accept help. Little progress was made. But my young friend, the doctor's wife, stuck with it for a year and a half, long after most would have given up. Then one day all of us were surprised when our poor broken friend stood up in the sharing period with her face radiantly aglow and said, "For the first time in my life, I like myself." The breakthrough of healing had come. She was a new person. She had been caught up in the faith and love of an intense caring group and had found healing. Let the Church be the Church!

A man who has meant much to me in my own spiritual growth was Dr. Albert Edward Day. Dr. Day was for years pastor in a great downtown Methodist Church in Baltimore, Maryland. There he had an intense prayer group which carried on a very effective healing ministry. Dr. Day would send patients to the doctors at Johns Hopkins for examination and confirmation of healing. The doctors would send patients to Dr. Day and his prayer group. It was an effective combination of medical skill plus faith and love. The results were surprising. Dr. Day followed the Master in being concerned about the problems of humanity, while, at the same time, channeling the healing love of God toward the hurts of individual persons.

Some were not healed, and Dr. Day recognized the mystery here — we do not yet see the whole picture. But it is an established fact that a group of dedicated, committed persons of faith, concentrating in love and prayer, are an effectual healing force.

In a large city church where I was serving we had such a prayer group. A woman from our church had to have difficult heart surgery. Our group was in deep prayer for her. Several of us were in the hospital during the operation. After surgery the leader of the heart team approached us gloomily. He said the tissues of the heart system were so weak they would not hold the stitches. The surgeons would have to go in again. He held out little hope. Our group continued to pray. After the second surgery the doctor came back to us amazed. He said that the situation was surprisingly different. Healing was taking place. She recovered and lived an active life for many more years. The doctors agreed that something had taken place beyond their skills.

For years I have held a Wednesday morning prayer service in our Chapel for personal needs and for healing. There is always somebody there, usually different people at different times. We read scripture, incidents from the healing ministry of Jesus. We pray. All come to the altar who have some special need. They tell us exactly what that need is. We lay hands on their heads one by one and pray for them specifically. Many people have been helped and this service has had a deepening influence upon the life of our congregation. By faith we are still in touch with the infinite love and healing power of God. And we know that Christ is present.

In recent years, sponsored by the American Cancer Society, I have spoken to several groups of cancer patients. For the most part, I find that these threatened people are growing in faith and love. They are an encouragement to me. They care for one another; they are aware of God; and they have hope for life here and life hereafter. In fact, they probably have a sense of wholeness beyond that of their neighbors. One thing I say to them is, "Don't ask, 'Why?' It cannot be fully answered. We do not, yet, see the whole picture. Your real answer is *your* response in *faith* to your illness. Wrap each other up with love and faith."

We are ever in the hands of God, and that is life.

While preaching recently in Topeka, Kansas, I sat in on a Biofeedback Seminar in the Menninger Clinic. It gives me great courage to see revealed the power of the subconscious mind on the functions of the body. Faith brings assurance to the subconscious mind, along with a definite healing effect on the body. The love and faith experience is a powerful form of energy. The universe is greater and more healing than we have ever supposed. Life is greater and more fulfilling than we have dared to expect. God is nearer and more caring than we have ever dared to believe.

Seek it and receive it. There are powers in our belief structure that we have never yet imagined. Can't you hear Jesus speaking on the housetop that night? "Listen to the wind, Nicodemas, listen to the wind." There are yet new dimensions of life for you.

In this expanded dimension of faith I begin to *know* some things, essential things: I know that I am forgiven, I know that I am loved with an infinite love. I know that I will pass into an unimaginable beauty of life and involvement beyond death. I *know* it.

God says, "Receive a new heart; receive a new spirit; receive a new wholeness. I have it waiting for you." Because of the experience of faith, certain healing factors (built into our systems by the Creator) now become operative, triggered by an inner assurance, and we are healed. The eminent physician, Dr. William Sadler, once said, "In neglecting prayer for healing we are neglecting the greatest single power in the healing of disease."

> Dear Heavenly Father:
>   I'm working on a puzzle,
>   pure and simple,
>   It is I.

> Dear searching child:
>   Here's the answer
>   to your puzzle,
>   pure and simple.
>   It is I.

— Ethelyn A. Shattuck

9

Why Fear Growing Old?

It is said that by the year 2000 one-half the population of our nation will be over 50 and one-third over 65 years of age. Those of us who are growing older will have plenty of company. We have a science, gerontology, dedicated to our well-being. We do not even have to surrender to senility: doctors tell us that it is not a normal state of old age; only 8 percent of older people need to fear such a breakdown. It is possible to remain alert and creative right down to the conclusion of our lives.

Marie Dressler once said, "It's not how old you are, but *how* you are old that counts." I remember hearing Dr. E. Stanley Jones speak just after his seventieth birthday. He said with great assurance, "God has just told me that I have ten more years of fruitful ministry." I said to myself that I would watch to see if this prophecy was fulfilled. I heard him speak again following his eightieth birthday, and he said, "God has told me that I still have some years of effective ministry." But he did not say how many. I believe that he continued his creative career until his 88th birthday.

Browning can still be trusted to give us the whole picture:

> Grow old along with me.
> The best is yet to be.
> The last of life, for which the first was made.
> Our times are in His Hand
> Who sayeth, 'A whole I planned,
> Youth shows but half; trust God; see all, nor be afraid!

And Edwin Markham gives us a vital cue:

> They who can smile when others hate,
> Nor bind the heart with frosts of fate,
> Their feet will go with laughter bold,
> The green roads of the Never-Old.

It's the *quality* of life that counts.

A vital Christian faith is, I believe, the greatest life-sustaining force as we face the increasing years of life. Isaiah 46:4 reveals the enduring undergirding structure of our lives: "Even to your old age I am he, even to your gray hairs I will carry you. I have made and I will bear, even I will carry and deliver you." It seems amazing that the Master of the Universe should care so much, and make each of us this personal guarantee. All we have to do is to "hang in there" by faith, and keep on living with purpose. Face it thoughtfully — has he ever really let you down? "I have made and and I will bear."

"A whole I planned, youth shows but half."

God is not a little boy playing games, jumping thoughtlessly from one thing to another, never finishing anything. What God starts he sees through. That means *us*, and that includes history.

"The whole wide world is in his hands." Yes!

Some who read these chapters will still be early in the process. What are the steps in life's total picture? First we skip across the low plains. There are innumerable paths; life seems endless. Next we climb the foothills. There is direction now, and there is pull and strain. But we cannot see the whole way. We pass through tunnels. It is dark. We are not sure where we will come out, but we trust the ultimate beckoning.

Now we reach the higher plains of marriage, family, vocation, commitment. The air is clearer, our vision better; there is beauty and meaning all around us. We can see backward and forward. There are more tunnels as we strive on toward the peaks of knowledge, aspiration, and service. And now above us, the final mountain pass — the Great Divide. Behind us, the life that was. Ahead of us, the life that is to be. Behold, The City of God! "I have made and I will carry. Even I will carry and deliver you."

Don't be afraid. Trust the whole process. "Don't worry about getting older;" says Burton Hillis, "when you stop getting older you are dead." Like the little boy said, "The day you're born, you're a gonner." No! God created us that we might share his life. It will take a whole lifetime of growing, stage by stage, to experience the life that

God has in mind for us here. Then we will be ready to begin the next step toward that which God has in mind for us, in that which lies beyond.

The Christian life is fulfillment, not decay. It goes forward, never backward. Only the years can bring the ripeness of maturity. Life with God is not going *into* a funnel; it is coming *out of* a funnel. This life does not shrivel and dwindle: it expands. The body weakens, the soul strengthens. Here lies the difference between man the animal and man the person of faith. The Christian is not afraid of the *upper half* of life. "I will carry and deliver you." Really, "the best *is* yet to be."

Emmett Fox strengthens us with his own experience of life: "I greet the unknown with a cheer, I press forward joyously, exulting in the Great Adventure . . . I have nothing to fear in life or death, because God is All . . ." Trusting, we seek to fulfill life, each year of it, one year at a time.

There is a grandeur about the way in which some persons of past generations faced life's impossible demands. Look at Grandmother as described by G. S. Childs:

> Grandmother, on a Winter's day,
> Milked the cows and fed them hay,
> Slopped the hogs, saddled the mule,
> And got the children off to school;
> Did a washing, mopped the floors,
> Washed the windows, and did the chores;
> Cooked a dish of home-dried fruit,
> Pressed her husband's Sunday suit,
> Swept the parlor, made the bed,
> Baked a dozen loaves of bread;
> Split some firewood, and lugged it in,
> Enough to fill the kitchen bin;
> Cleaned the lamps and put in oil,
> Stewed some apples she thought would spoil,
> Cooked a supper that was delicious,
> And afterward washed up all the dishes;
> Fed the cat and sprinkled the clothes,
> Mended a basketful of hose;
> Then opened the organ and began to play,
> When you *Come to the End of a Perfect Day*.
>
> — G. S. Childs

Courage and faith and a sense of humor can still sustain us.

In addition to this, Grandmother had an indominable faith that supported her day by day:

> He giveth more grace when the burdens are greater.
> He sendeth more strength when the labors increase,
> To added afflictions he addeth his mercy.
> To multiplied trials he multiplies peace.
> When we have exhausted our store of endurance,
> When our strength has failed ere day is half done,
> When we reach the end of our hoarded resources,
> Our Father's full giving is only begun.
> His love has no limit, his grace has no measure.
> His power no boundary known unto men,
> For out of his infinite riches in Jesus,
> He giveth and giveth and giveth again.

She really believed it and was sustained by its truth.

But some of the old timers didn't have the stuff that Grandmother was made of. MacRae, in a *Reader's Digest* article, tells of observing an old fellow sitting on a flour barrel in a country store. Someone mentioned that this ancient one was more than a 100 years old. "Amazing," exclaimed MacRae. "We don't see nothing amazing about that," one of the neighbors replied. "All he's done is grow old, and he's taken a lot longer than most folks to do that." A person of faith does much more than just pile up the years. After all of his great accomplishments, someone said of the aging Leo Tolstoy, "He, himself, was his own greatest production." He died, still seeking, still learning.

Some people really "blow it." Maybe it's a sickness of youth they have never thrown off. Margaret Fishback gives expression to this sadness:

> The older I grow
>   The meaner I get.
> Don't tell me, I know
> The older I grow,
> Like peanuts and snow,
>   Like gossip and debt,
> The older I grow
>   The meaner I get.

Schindler, in his book, *How to Live 365 Days a Year*, writes: "Many people handle age poorly, simply because they have never handled any part of their lives well." Bad habits get worse; the effects of wrong living pile up; raw dispositions become more raw. But on the positive side, we could go along with *Cheerful Cherub*:

Age has the lightest touch
Upon the kind of face
Where ghosts of many smiles
Have left a gentle trace.

But how do you counterbalance the destructive characteristics with positive qualities? As you prepare for life you are preparing for age. "Every day is Judgment Day." We are becoming what we are going to be.

The best approach to age is to deepen one's life now, to improve the disposition, to control the temper, to sweeten the spirit, to deepen one's consciousness of God, to give life freely so that we may receive it. We can prepare ourselves financially and emotionally, in interests, in spirit, and in friendships. We can be increasingly proud of what life is doing for us, to us, and through us.

Perhaps some life begins at sixty-five rather than forty. One doesn't retire from life. We retire from one phase of responsibilities to new dimensions of creativity, interests, and service. We are not just "getting ready for death." Relaxed, new, creative, we are preparing for life. We are not going to play golf and bridge forever; we seek a balance of recreation and involvement. I have knowledge; I have wisdom; I have vision; I have talents; these are stimulated by faith and compassion. I intend still to be contributing to life and enjoying it. I am sustained and challenged by my new interests.

A man of seventy was sick and about to give up. His doctors put him in a nursing home where they put him in charge of drama and staging. He had knowledge, and he discovered that he had gifts. He was happy. He got well and lived ten more years — a happy, creative, joyous life. If I "retire" from life, I am moving away from God; when I am creatively *involved* in life, I move toward God.

Harry Emerson Fosdick, speaking to a group of Senior Citizens, said, "You made a fairly clean hit in youth . . . you got to first base, ran to second; today you are on third; and you are going to be caught napping off third when all your friends are expecting you to get home." Let's finish the game!

"I do my job," writes Emmet Fox, "and pass on to another. I am going to live forever; in a thousand years from now I shall be alive and active somewhere — a 100 thousand thousand years. Always the future will be better than the present or the past, because I am growing and progressing. I am an immortal soul." He got the point of the promise, "I have made and I will bear, I will carry and deliver you — even to your old age."

To Grandma Moses and others, "Life begins at eighty." Bishop Welch was writing and speaking creatively and with conviction when he was 103. Lyman Abbot was a leading editor at eighty-six. Charles Elliott was an outstanding educator at ninety-two. Gladstone was Prime Minister of Great Britain at eighty-three. Tennyson wrote "Crossing the Bar" at eighty-three. Socrates began taking dancing lessons at seventy. And Ronald Reagan became President of the United States pushing seventy. There can be great joy and accomplishment in the older years.

"I was never happier," writes George Santayana, the philosopher, "never happier than I am now. The charm I find in old age comes of having learned to live in the moment, and therefore in Eternity; and this means recovering a perpetual youth, since nothing can be fresher than each day as it dawns and changes." Lord Roberts, as an old man, revealed the same understanding of life when he said to the artist painting his portrait, "Don't erase my lines — I won them."

On his sixty-ninth birthday, President Faunce, of Brown University, gave the whole picture in these words, "The long succession of birthdays brings me to the sensation of being lifted by an elevator through the successive floors of some lofty building. On each floor the horizon is wider, the sunlight brighter, the distant and inaccessible things seem nearer."

Maude Roydon approached age with a unique outlook: "Do not desire to die in harness . . . desire to see the whole of life . . . to miss old age is to miss something natural, beautiful and right." Quintus Quiz asked for "a little time apart, so that I might collect my soul before I go into the other world." Or it might even be as the little girl said of her grandmother, whom she saw reading her Bible constantly, "Granny's cramming for the finals." Karle Wilson Baker opens the window upon a beautiful possibility for all of us:

Let me grow lovely, growing old —
     So many fine things do: . . .
Laces and ivory and gold
     And silks need not be new.
There is healing in old trees,
     Old streets a glamour hold.
Why may not I, as well as these,
     Grow lovely, growing old?"

All of us are borne on the bosom of the river. All of us are seeking home, and home is God. As young men just out of college, a friend and I bought a "T" model Ford and went West to work the wheat fields. At times we were hungry and lonely. Early one morning, while sleeping on the ground in the "Bad Lands" of the Dakotas, my friend and I had a strange experience. I woke up with a strong feeling that there were three of us there rather than two. The perception was vivid and real, perceived not as a threat but as a feeling of peace and protection. Later we packed up and resumed our journey. Both of us were unusually quiet. Then I revealed to my friend my strange experience. He was shocked, and said to me. "I had the same vivid experience. But I didn't tell you. I thought you might not understand."

Neither of us forgot this experience. It was real. Someone was there. Who? My mother who was in heaven? My father, who was probably praying for us early in the morning? Or a sense of the presence of God, who is always with us, and makes his presence known again and again? At any rate, two young men, a long way from home, learned a lesson for life — *we are never alone!* He is with us all the way — "Even to your gray hairs" — and then, "The City of God!"

Through joys and through sorrows, through afflictions and through peace, in youth and in mature years, we find life's fulfillment in God, who is the same yesterday, today , and forever. And Christ says: "Go, go, keep going in life's compassionate involvement — and I will be with you always, even to the end."

John Haynes Holmes adds his touch of vision:

Thou wilt not lose nor leave us,
     Thy love endureth still;
Patient and calm and changeless

Abides Thy holy will.
Thine are we till the ages
Outwatch the farthest sun,
And men at last in gladness
Proclaim, Thy will be done!

10

Life After Life

An author writing in *Vogue* magazine says that he believes America's loss of values, and her moral and ethical breakdown, arise from the fact that for the first time in history most of the people of America do not believe in life after death. When we lose our faith we lose our focus on a dependable structure of life. If life has no meaning, if it is going nowhere, then we can summarize history and the future, — "So What?" Eat, drink, and be merry — if you can! If life after death is *not*, I don't want to believe in it. If it *is* true, I want to fit my life style to the full dimensions of my being.

Suddenly, the medical profession is getting interested in *Death and Dying* (Dr. Elizabeth Kubler-Ross) and *Life After Life* (Dr. Raymond A. Moody). The center of my faith is still based on what God has revealed to us through the centuries, and in the resurrection of Christ. But in a time when many have lost faith, God seems to be reminding us of Truth through a new medium. God must be saying, "They are not developing their faith; they are looking more and more to science for a way of life. Therefore, I will speak to them through science and turn them back to their faith."

Dr. Kubler-Ross writes of Dr. Rymond Moody's book concerning what people experience after death: "It is research such as Dr. Moody presents in his book that will enlighten many and will confirm what we have been taught for two thousand years — that there is life after death . . . It is evident from his findings that the dying patient continues to have a conscious awareness of his environment after being pronounced clinically dead."

By coincidence, Dr. Moody was made aware of the fact that two or three patients, first pronounced dead but later revived, had had almost identical experiences while they were clinically dead. This challenged Dr. Moody to comb the country, seeking out persons — old, young, educated, uneducated — who had had a death experience. He interviewed over a hundred of these and was amazed to discover that their experiences were almost identical. As a result, he wrote his book!

We should not treat Dr. Moody's book as a complete picture. These persons who had been clinically dead from five to twenty-six minutes were all resuscitated. They had only a glimpse of the After Life. Theirs is perhaps a glimpse of the Narthex of Heaven. But they were sure they had been there and had experienced its reality and its spirit.

According to Dr. Moody, what did they experience? There were minor variations, but the general structure of the experience was the same for each: The dying person hears himself pronounced dead by the doctor. He seems to float up against the ceiling. He is very alert and alive. He watches the team of doctors as they struggle to resuscitate him. Later he can tell them exactly what they did and the procedures they used. The patient can see loved ones in other parts of the hospital and know what they are saying.

Then there is a noise, like wind blowing. They are drawn into a tunnel of darkness, but almost immediately can see the light at the other end. They break out into this light and experience the presence of a Person in the Light. They feel loved and accepted. They experience a joy and a freedom never known before. In the presence of the Person in the Light their whole life flows rapidly before their vision in intense detail, like a full-color, high-speed film. Much of the life they see they would like to change. The Person in the Light asks them if they have had a good life, if they are ready to leave, if they have learned to love as they are now being loved. They glimpse dimensions of life and love they had never dreamed of.

One person, who had attempted to commit suicide, found himself in a place of darkness. He knew that he had missed life and wanted to come back.

All these persons could see some kind of barrier, a stream, a shore, a fence, a canyon. On the other side they saw loved ones who had died. They recognized them and were recognized by them. Their loved ones were beckoning them to come on.

At this time these persons were turned back. They didn't want to go back. They had never seen life like this before; they wanted to stay. But they were resuscitated. They returned to the body to pick up all its old pains and responsibilities. They wanted to tell others, but nobody seemed to understand. They wanted to help others. They wanted to live out the new dimensions of life that they had experienced.

One woman tried to tell her minister. He said, "You have been hallucinating." She shut up and didn't try again. After reading Raymond Moody's book, a doctor said to his wife, "I have been on resuscitating teams, and nobody has told me tales like these." She answered, "Honey, you remember I had an experience like this. I wanted to tell you, but I didn't think you would understand."

The whole life of these persons now is affected by this experience. Their relationships are different. They have a new attitude toward life and death. They aren't afraid anymore. They know they were not ready to die and they want to become ready. They have a completely new understanding of love. Caring and compassion seem now, to be the central meaning of life.

It seemed to them that God loved all of them. Perhaps he loved some of them with sadness because they were rejecting life, some of them with gladness because they were accepting life.

What did some of these persons say about their experience?

"I was trying to get to that light at the end of the darkness because I felt that it was Christ . . . It was not a frightening experience . . . I said to myself, 'If this is it, if I am to die, then I know who waits for me at the end, there in that light.' "

Another said, "The thought came to my mind, 'Lovest thou me? Do you really love me?' I was surrounded by overwhelming love."

Another: "In this light I saw the mean little things I had done as a child . . . I wished that I hadn't done these things, and I wished I could go back and undo them."

A Mother: "The Lord sent me back . . . I definitely felt him there, and I knew that he recognized me. And yet he didn't see fit to let me into heaven . . . I believe it was because I had those two small children to raise, or because I just wasn't personally ready to be there."

A high school boy: "I was a typical high schoool fraternity brat . . . after this happened to me, I wanted to know more . . . I felt I had aged over-night . . . I kept thinking, 'There is so much I've got to find out . . . There's more to life than Friday night movies and the football game. And there's more to me that I don't even know about' . . . I started thinking, 'What is the limit of the human being and of the mind?' It just opened up a whole new world."

Another: "It seems I'm more in tune with people now." And another, in the same vein: "I can sense the needs in other individuals' lives . . . I have been with people in the elevator . . . I can almost read their faces, and tell that they need help, and what kind." And another with new insights: "I don't feel bad at funerals any more. I kind of rejoice at them, because I know what the dead person is passing through."

A man, who had adopted his nephew who was on drugs, heard the Person in the Light say, "Since you are asking for someone else, I will let you go back. You will live until you have seen your nephew become a man."

Dr. Moody concludes the book: "What we learn about death may make an important difference in the way we live our lives . . . These events have profound implications for what every one of us is doing with our life . . . We cannot fully understand this life until we catch a glimpse of what lies beyond it."

Once I caught a glimpse of this Light. I knew for a moment this unutterable peace, this being loved, this absence of threat, this total freedom, this absolute assurance. I believe it was for me a glimpse of the Eternal. It shall forever beckon me onward.

I was fortunate to know Dudley and Alice Ward. Dr. Ward headed the area of Social Concerns for the United Methodist Church at the National level. They were both outstanding individuals of unusual intelligence, training and leadership ability. For this reason I was deeply impressed by their book, *I Remain Unvanquished.*

Alice Ward was struck down by cancer. In the early stages of the disease, she had a death experience. She saw Christ; she wanted to stay in that other world. But Christ said (a loose quotation), "Alice, I need you in the City of Washington. There are many people there who need your help. You will be able to see their need and help them in deep and lasting ways, for my sake."

For about nine years she had an unusual Ministry of Counseling in and around the City of Washington. She could see into people's minds and problems and could minister to those problems in a unique manner. She and Dudley grew amzingly in Spirit and depth and experience.

Alice wrote forcefully about all this until her death. Dudley picked the story up and wrote the last chapter. Alice died beautifully early in the morning. Dudley, who had been attending her, sat in the room for thirty minutes before calling her doctors. The room was full of Presence. It seemed that all of their loved ones who had gone to heaven had gathered there. There was a strange aliveness.

When the two doctors came, fifteen minutes apart, their reactions were surprisingly the same. As Dudley met them at the door, they exclaimed, "Dr. Ward, what goes on here? This house is alive. It is filled with life."

I rejoice that we can keep the benefits of our scientific knowledge and at the same time rediscover the ultimate and the immediate reality of the Spirit. This is where life finds its final consummation; otherwise, there is no meaning.

J. B. Phillips, the well-known British New Testament scholar and friend of C. S. Lewis, shares an experience in his book, *For This Day*. He was near death in the hospital. Apparently he was in a coma. He could make no response of any sort. Not an eyelash could he move to indicate that he was conscious. Yet he was totally alert and was aware of all that went on around him. He asked himself how he could be alive, and yet be able to make no response to life. That night at ten p.m., when his doctor came by to check on him, he heard him say to the nurse, "Dr. Phillips will not be with us in the morning. He cannot make it through the night." There he lay, totally aware, wanting to shake his head, "No, No!" but could make no response.

That night he had a vision. He was on a hillside in the midst of an immense junk yard. There were old machines, old rotten lumber, decaying tires, old rusty cars, broken-down farm machinery. Dr. Phillips was struggling desperately to get out of this prison of junk and ruin. As he struggled and strained and made little progress, he glanced across at the opposite hill and saw perfect life and beauty — blue sky, soft clouds, green grass, birds singing, joyful people singing and laughing.

He strained all the harder to reach that new land. Finally he reached the little stream that separated the two hills. There was a little bridge across the stream, and he was overjoyed as he put his foot on the bridge to cross it. It was then that he looked up and saw Christ standing in the middle of the bridge, looking down at him. Christ was smiling but was quietly shaking his head. With broken heart Phillips realized he could not cross. But he made an unforgettable observation: "There stood Christ, and he looked upon me with *total compassion* and *absolute authority*." (What a marvelous balance of opposite qualities!)

There was no question: he had to go back. He woke up crying, as though his heart would break. The nurse rushed in and asked, "Dr. Phillips, why are you crying? You have passed your crisis. You are going to get well." But he said, "I could not tell her. She would not have understood."

Then, Phillips adds, "That was forty years ago. But to this day I am absolutely certain that that night I touched Reality." I, too, believe that he did.

I recall what Paul experienced as he watched over the clothes of those who stoned Stephen to death. Stephen was seeing something Real. He cried out, "Behold I see the heavens opened and the Son of Man standing at the right hand of God." His face glowed in the reflected light of what he was seeing. Paul never forgot that light until he saw it himself on the road to Damascus.

Emanuel Swedenburg, who lived in Stockholm, from 1688 to 1772 describes his experience as "the 'Light of the Lord' which permeates the hereafter, a light of ineffable brightness which I have glimpsed myself."

Malcolm Muggeridge tells of the death of William Blake, genius, scientist, artist, and poet, who died in 1827: "Blake lay in bed, a friend who was there recalled, singing songs so divinely, so beautifully, that Catherine (his wife) got up to listen better, and then he turned to her and said, 'They are not mine, you know,' and repeated it more emphatically, 'They are not mine.' Then he went on to tell her that they would never be parted, and that after he was dead he would continue to watch over her just as he had during the years of their long companionship . . .

"He went on singing in his bed in the same divine way until about six in the evening, and then, as he said in one of his poems, silently, invisibly, the human spirit left him, becoming a part of the eternity on which his eyes had been so faithfully set during his mortal years."

Muggeridge quotes a friend of Kierkegaard, one who was present at his death in 1855. The friend said he had a look about him that "shone out from a sublime and blessed splendor which seemed to me to make the whole room light. Everything was concentrated in those eyes as the source of light, heartfelt love, blissful dissolution of sadness, penetrating clearness of mind, and a jesting smile."

Again Muggeridge quotes Bonhoeffer as he wrote just before he was executed in a Nazi Prison: "You must never doubt that I'm traveling with gratitude and cheerfulness along the road where I am being led. My past life is brim-full of God's goodness, and my sins are covered by the forgiving love of Christ crucified."

I quote these death scenes because I believe that they reveal an authentic glimpse of the reality on the other side of death. We can be assured. We need not be afraid.

For us, the focus is on Jesus' dying words: "Father into thy hands I commend my spirit." We draw assurance from the Resurrection scene in Matthew. There was a Divine impertinence about it. The awful power of Rome had "closed out" the Jesus story. *But!* But "An angel descended from heaven and *rolled away* the stone, and *sat on it*. And his face shone like lightning. And the strong, fierce Roman guards (the full Military Power of that day) lay like dead men.

"But the angel said to the women, 'You have nothing to fear. Come look, he is not here. He is risen. Go tell his Disciples.' And as they went, Jesus met them in the path." (A paraphrase)

The front door of the tomb opens upon this life. But the back door opens upon the Eternal. There are two doors. Be not afraid! God is in charge here! You have just come home.

I believe that Christ is the Being of Light. He loves us. He is waiting for us there. I am not afraid to go where Christ has gone.

Death is the last of life's traumatic experiences and Christ has conquered it. "This is the Victory, even our faith."

There is a small book that comes out of England, *God at Eventide*. Two elderly English women have given themselves to concentrated prayerful listening every evening. They write down what they hear the Master saying.

This is one of the messages they pass on to us. I believe it could be a word from Christ to us at this moment of the world's history:

> "Persons are trying to live the Christian life in the light and teaching of my three years' mission alone. That was never my purpose.
> "I came to reveal my Father, to show the God-Spirit working in man. I taught not that man was only to attempt to copy Jesus of Nazareth, but that man was also to be possessed by my Spirit, the Spirit actuating all that I did, that man would be inspired (indwelt) as I was."

"Help me, God! It's hard to cope!"

"I know it's difficult sometimes. But you *can* cope, for I am *with* you. My Spirit is *within* you. Now all things are possible."